PRESS OUT AND BUILD
SUPERBIKE

Published by Top That! Publishing plc
Tide Mill Way, Woodbridge, Suffolk, IP12 1AP, UK
www.topthatpublishing.com
Copyright © 2011 Top That! Publishing plc
All rights reserved.
2 4 6 8 9 7 5 3
Printed and bound in China

SUPERBIKE RACING

Superbike racing is one of the most exciting sports in the world. Many fans of the sport make long journeys to experience the thrill of watching their favourite riders and teams up close.

A photo finish

Some people claim to have seen Superbike racing in California in the early 1970s. Officially though, the first ever Superbike championship was held at Daytona International Speedway on 5th March 1976. It was arranged by the American Motorcycle Organisation.

Prior to the 1970s, motorcycles were far more basic.

When American rider Steve McLaughlin and Englishman Reg Pridmore raced their identical Butler and Smith BMWs across the finish line, officials had to check photographs before the winner could be declared. The photos showed that McLaughlin's machine was just a few inches ahead of Pridmore's when it crossed the line.

Riders then started racing on tracks using ordinary street bikes, which were very powerful but difficult to handle in race conditions.

To solve this problem, a style of racing was developed where riders take corners with one knee held out, their bike sliding under its massive weight.

Racing in Europe

Traditional European motorcycle racing took place on the road. Typically, machines were small, handled very well and skilful riders were able to take corners at great speed.

Modern superbikes can really be thrown around the track.

WHAT IS A SUPERBIKE?

Initially, there was some confusion over what a Superbike was. It meant different things in different countries around the world.

All in agreement

It has now been agreed that Superbikes must be built from production road bikes (bikes sold to and ridden by the general public), but can be supercharged for racing. There are three weight classes:

- 750 cc, 4 cylinders – 159 kg
- 900 cc, 3 cylinders – 162 kg
- 1000 cc, 2 cylinders – 164 kg

Going international

In the mid to late '70s in the UK a series of Transatlantic Trophy events took place, pulling huge crowds.

Before Superbike there had been other world championships based on the idea of big bikes racing separately from the established grand prix races. Events were held, such as Tourist Trophy Formula 1,

Legendary rider Carl Fogarty at the helm of his Ducati.

inspired when the Isle of Man TT race lost its status as a grand prix.

By 1980, American Superbike had become the racing class for Daytona. Whilst European riders raced at Daytona, European fans weren't really aware of Superbike racing. As the momentum towards a truly international Superbike championship built, the big motorcycle production factories got in on the act, and Ducati, Yamaha and Kawasaki started to produce more and more sophisticated bikes.

Competitors at the start of a Superbike race.

COMPETITIONS

The first World Superbike Championships took place in 1988. The first race was held at Donington Park in England on 3rd April. It was won by Marco Lucchinelli of Italy, riding for Ducati.

Changing times

By 2002, all of the major motorbike manufacturers were entering their finest production bikes into the World Superbike Championships.

Race authorities agreed to allow 1000 cc four-cylinder bikes to race in the Championships and compete against 750 cc single-engined bikes. However, these 1000 cc bikes had to have air restrictors fitted in order to limit their speed and keep the competition fair.

A sleek 750 cc Sport Ducati.

Carl Fogarty

Ducati is one of the most successful teams in the World Superbike Championships, and Carl Fogarty is one of Ducati's most successful racers.

Fogarty won his first World Superbike race at Donington in 1992, on a Ducati Sports Motorcycle 888. Before this, he had won the world TTF1 championships twice and three Isle of Man TT's.

Carl Fogarty, nicknamed 'King' or 'Foggy'.

Fogarty's record of four World Superbike Championships, in 1994, '95, '98 and '99, and 59 race wins (55 on Ducati) will take some beating!

In 2000, Fogarty was forced to retire from racing when he suffered serious injuries in an accident at the Phillip Island Circuit in Australia.

MOTORCYCLE RACING

Ever since motorcycles were first invented, riders have had the desire to race them against one another. Nowadays, motorcycle racing takes place all around the world.

First race

In September 1896, eight competitors took part in a race from Paris to Nantes and back. This is the first recorded motorcycle race. The course covered 152 km (139 miles), and the winner was M. Chevalier on a Michelin-Dion tricycle. His winning time was 4 hours, 10 minutes and 37 seconds.

The governing body for motorcycling in Britain, the Auto-Cycle Union (ACU) was founded in 1903. The Fédération Internationale Motorcycliste (FIM) was created in 1904. Today the FIM is the world governing body.

Until the outbreak of World War II in 1939, most of the fastest vehicles on the road were British. Italian motorcycles, such as Guzzi, Garelli, Gilera, and MV Agusta, then took over, until the Germans introduced their consistently high-performing BMW.

From the 1970s onwards, Japanese teams, including Honda, Yamaha, Suzuki and Kawasaki, were the consistent winners – and very popular on the street too.

Apart from some rare occasions, like Ducati's domination of the World Superbike Championships, Japanese manufacturers lead the way today.

John Surtees winning the 1959 Isle of Man Junior TT on an MV Augusta.

DIFFERENT TYPES

There are many different types of motorcycle racing, which take place on different surfaces, outside and in stadiums.

Dirt-track racing

Riders race to the finish of this dirt-track race.

In America, riders race powerful bikes on mile-long (1.6 km) oval tracks with dirt surfaces, which is why Americans call this type of racing dirt-track racing.

Ice speedway riders lean into a corner.

Speedway

Speedway bikes are lightweight machines without brakes, which race on rough surfaces, indoors and out. Races usually take place with up to four riders, racing four laps anti-clockwise around the track. The first rider over the finishing line is the winner.

Ice speedway

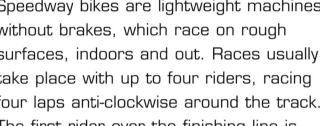

One of the most exciting, but dangerous, versions of speedway is ice speedway. Riders race on ice with specially modified tyres. This kind of speedway usually takes place in extremely cold parts of Europe, such as Sweden, Norway, Denmark and Finland, for example.

Riders racing in the sand on Le Touquet beach in France.

Scrambling

Riders taking part in scrambling, or motocross, are judged on their ability to race over a fixed distance or within a specified time. Races often take place over difficult terrain – the muddier the better!

Long-track racing

In Europe, there is a type of motorcycle racing called long-track racing. These races take place over sand, shale or grass on oval tracks that have been used for horse-trotting races. It is also known as 1,000 m racing, because this is the distance around the track.

Italian Superbike champion Marco Lucchinelli.

Observation trials

Observation trials are events where the riders have to get around a difficult course without touching the ground with any part of the body. The course is divided into sections, which contain different hazards, from bumps and slippery surfaces on outdoor courses to man-made obstacles set up in stadiums.

Superbike racing on the Isle of Man.

Time trials

Time trials are similar to observation trials. They are cross-country events in which riders are given route and time cards to be stamped at control points around the course. For every two minutes that a rider is late at a control point they lose a point, so the rider with the fewest penalty points wins the event.

Drag-racing

In drag-racing, two riders race specially prepared bikes over 400 m (a quarter of a mile). The winner gets through to the next round.

Road racing

Road races are held over closed public roads, or on specially built circuits which include features normally found on public roads.

The first motor race to be held on the Isle of Man took place in 1904. The Manx government decided to allow motor racing to take place on the island's public roads – something that wasn't possible in England.

In 1907, the first TT Tourist Trophy race was held on the Isle of Man Short Course. Racing moved to the 61 km (38 miles) Mountain Circuit in 1911.

The sidecar passenger leans dangerously into corners.

Sidecar racing

The passenger taking part in sidecar racing has to be extremely skilled, knowing which way to lean when the bike takes a corner in order to keep it on the track.

Sprinting

Sprinting is a run against the clock over a straight course up to 1.6 km (1 mile) long, although the usual distance is 400 m (a quarter of a mile).

Bob McIntyre was the first to reach 100 mph around the TT circuit.

The motorcycle is put together in number order: starting with 1, moving to 2 and so on. All dotted lines indicate scored edges which are to be folded. When instructions refer to the left or right of the motorcycle, you should assume that it is facing you. Adult help may be required.

1. Take the Left Engine and Top Frame pieces. Holding them face up, bend down all the scored edges.

2. Attach the Left Engine piece to the Top Frame by slotting the tab numbered 1 into slot 1 on the Left Engine.

Make sure that once the tabs are through the slots, the small tabs on either side are opened up to secure it in place.

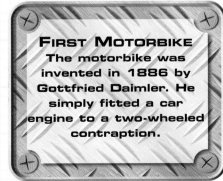

FIRST MOTORBIKE
The motorbike was invented in 1886 by Gottfried Daimler. He simply fitted a car engine to a two-wheeled contraption.

3. Push tab 2 into slot 2 on the Top Frame. Then insert tab 3 on the Top Frame into slot 3 on the Left Engine piece.

Make sure you bend the shape of the edges to make the contour of the Top Frame.

4. Now take the Right Engine piece and, holding it face up, bend down all the scored edges.

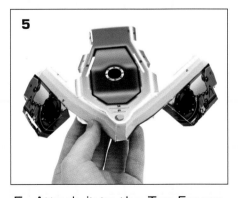

5. Attach it to the Top Frame by pushing tabs 4, 5 and 6 into their respective slots.

OLDEST RIDER
Briton Fergus Anderson is the oldest rider to have won a 500 cc grand prix. He was 44 years old when he won the 1953 Spanish grand prix on a Moto Guzzi.

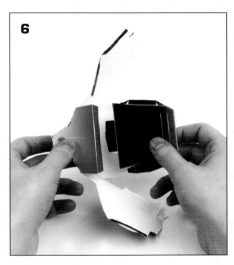

6. Take the Radiator and bend down all scored lines. Fix the Radiator to the bottom of the Top Frame by pushing tab 7 into slot 7.

7. Secure the Radiator in place by pushing tabs 8 and 9 into their respective slots.

WORLD FAMOUS
The world famous TT Motorcycle Races have been held on the Isle of Man since 1907.

8. Press out the Bottom Frame. Bend down all the scored edges and fix it to the Left Engine piece by pushing tab 10 into slot 10.

At this stage also push tab 11 on the Top Frame into slot 11 on the Left Engine.

Tab 12 on the Bottom Frame goes into slot 12 on the Top Frame.

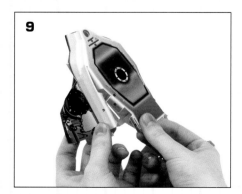

9. Push tab 13 on the Top Frame into slot 13 on the Right Engine and tab 14 on the Bottom Frame into slot 14 on the Top Frame.

10. Push tab 15 on the Right Engine into slot 15 on the Bottom Frame to lock the main structure of the motorcycle in place.

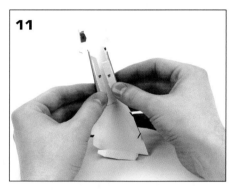

11. Take the Exhaust pipe and bend down all scored edges to make it flexible.

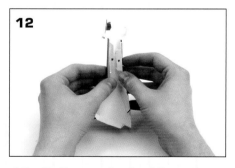

12. Pull round tab 16 and place into slot 16 to form a tube shape.

Make sure you open out the small tabs once the tab is through the slot to secure. You may need a pencil to access the inside of the tube.

Push tab 17 through slot 17 on the Exhaust Pipe too.

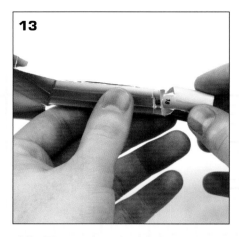

13. To push tab 18 into slot 18 you will have to push it up at an angle of 45°.

14. Take the Rear Exhaust Pipe and bend down all the scored edges to make it flexible.

Curl it into a tube shape to fix tab 19 into slot 19.

MOST WINS
Giacomo Agostini has won more 500 cc grand prix than any other rider. He won 68 times between 1965 and 1976. The next best is Mick Doohan with 54.

15. To close the ends of the tube on the Rear Exhaust Pipe, fold in tabs 20 and 21 and push them into their respective slots.

16. Attach the Rear Exhaust Pipe to the Exhaust Pipe by pushing tabs 22 and 23 into their respective slots.

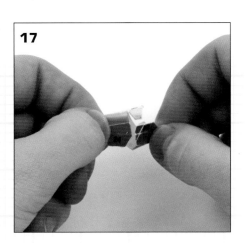

17. Take the Exhaust Pipe End. Wrap it around and fix into place by pushing slots numbered 24 into each other.

18. To fix this onto the Rear Exhaust Pipe just push tabs 25 and 26 into slots 25 and 26.

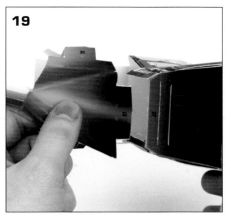

19. Fit the whole exhaust onto the Radiator by pushing tab 27 into slot 27.

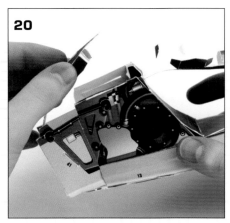

20. On the Bottom Frame, tabs 28 and 29 are pushed into slots 28 and 29 on the Right and Left Engine pieces.

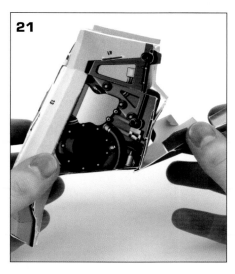

21. Pull the whole exhaust pipe up towards the Bottom Frame and secure it by pushing tab 30 into slot 30 and tab 31 into slot 31.

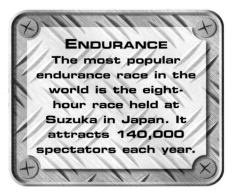

ENDURANCE
The most popular endurance race in the world is the eight-hour race held at Suzuka in Japan. It attracts 140,000 spectators each year.

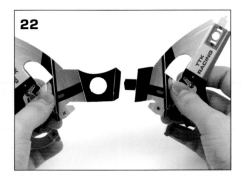

22. Take the Left Swinging Arm and Right Swinging Arm and push the scored edges down to make the pieces more flexible.

Put them together by pushing tab 32 into slot 32.

23

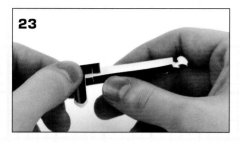

23. Press out the side stand. Hold it face up and push down all the scored edges to make it flexible.

Wrap around the end piece to form an 'L' shape and push both slots numbered 33 into each other.

24

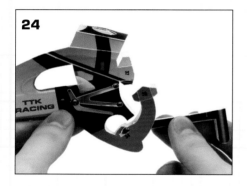

24. Hold the Swinging Arm which was previously formed by both left and right pieces and bring in the sides.

Place the hooks numbered 34 and 35 on the Side Stand into the slots numbered 34 and 35. These must be put in from the inside of the panels.

FAMOUS TEAMS
Famous teams in World Superbikes include Ducati, Honda, Aprilia, Kawasaki, Yamaha and Suzuki.

25

25. Attach this whole assembly to the Bottom Frame by pushing tabs 36 and 37 into the slots numbered 36 and 37.

At this stage, push tabs 38 and 39 into their slots too.

26

26. Hold the Rear Frame piece face up and bend down the scored edges.

Fix this to the Bottom Frame by pushing tab 40 into slot 40 and tab 41 into slot 41 on the other side.

27

27. Tab 42 on the Rear Frame pushes into slot 42 on the Rear Exhaust.

SPEED
500 cc bikes can get up to 322 km/h (200 mph) on the straights.

28

28. Hold the Fuel Tank face up and push down all the scored edges in order to make it flexible.

Begin by folding back the tabs of both parts numbered 43 onto themselves.

Then slide these two newly folded parts under each other until you can't see the tabs.

To lock it into place, unfold the tabs on the inside. Repeat this process with tabs numbered 44.

29

29. To form the shape of the tank, push tabs 45, 46, 47 and 48 into their respective slots.

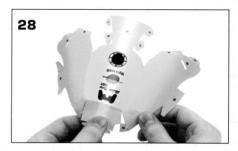

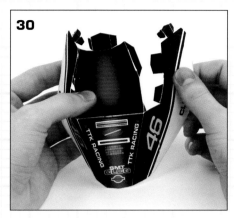

30. Press out the seat and make sure that all the scored pieces on the Seat piece are folded down.

Take tabs 49 and 50 and push them into slots 49 and 50, remembering to open up the small tabs once through the slot.

31. Tabs 51, 52 and 53 on the Seat all push into their respective slots on the Fuel Tank.

BIG JUMP
In 1978 eighteen year-old stunt rider Eddie Kidd jumped his bike over fourteen double decker buses, a distance of 58 m (190 ft).

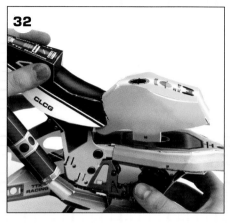

32. Fix the Fuel Tank onto the Top Frame by pushing tabs 54, 55 and 56 into slots 54, 55 and 56.

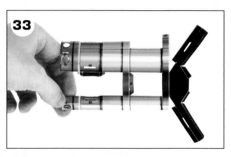

33. Hold the Front Forks piece face up and bend down the scored edges.

To form the tube shape of the forks, wrap the card around and push tab 57 into slot 57 and tab 58 into slot 58.

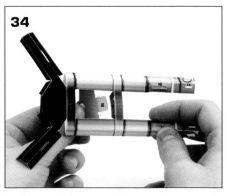

34. Find the Steering Connector. Push tab 59 into the slot numbered 59 on the Front Forks.

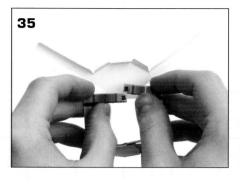

35. Slots 60 on the Front Forks just slide into each other to secure in place.

KNEEPADS
Motorcycle racers can touch the ground with their knees when cornering. They must therefore wear really strong pads to protect their knees.

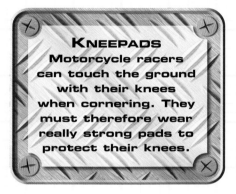

36. Take the Front Mud Guard piece and bend down all scored edges to make it flexible.

Begin by folding back the tabs of both parts numbered 61 onto themselves. Then slide these two newly folded parts under each other until you can't see the tabs. To lock into place, unfold the tabs on the inside.

Repeat with tabs 62.

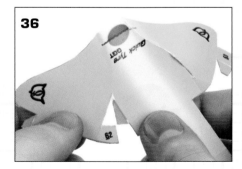

IDENTIFICATION
Each bike is identified by a number which can be clearly seen. Bikes will also be painted in the team's colours.

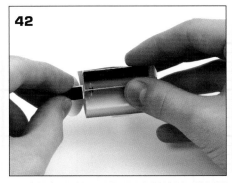

39. Take the Front Steering Pin (number 66) and bend it along the score lines into a squared off tube.

Use this to secure the Front Forks to the motorcycle frame by pushing it through the hole at the front of the frame, then through the hole in the Steering Connector.

Open up the ends to stop it falling through the hole.

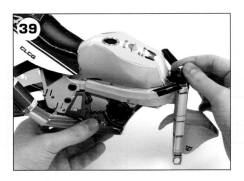

42. Close the ends by taking in tabs 69 and 70 over and into their own end of the tube.

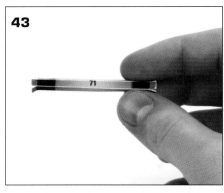

43. Take the piece numbered 71 (the Rear Wheel Pin) and form a square-sided tube by folding in all the scored edges.

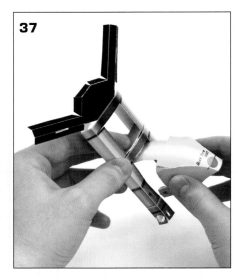

37. To attach the Front Mud Guard onto the Front Forks, push tabs 63 and 64 into their respective slots.

40. Tab 67 on the Handlebar Support tucks over to push into slot 67 on the black handlebars.

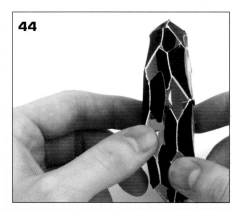

44. To make the Back Wheel take both parts and, holding them face up, bend down all the scored edges.

Fix the two pieces together by interlocking all the tabs around the edge of the tyre.

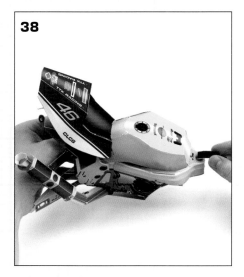

38. To attach the Handlebar Support piece push tab 65 into slot 65 on the Top Frame.

41. Make the Rear Wheel Drum by pushing slots 68 into each other to form a tube shape.

45. Push the Rear Wheel Drum through the hole in the centre of the wheel, making sure that it fits centrally within it.

Push the Back Wheel Chain piece against the right-hand side of the wheel and the Back Wheel Disc against the left-hand side of the wheel.

46. Secure them in place by pushing through the Rear Wheel Pin (number 71) made in Step 43.

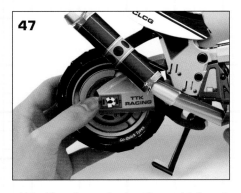

47. Fix the whole Rear Wheel onto the Swinging Arms by pushing the Rear Wheel Pin through the small holes.

Open up the ends of the pin to secure it in place.

48. To cover the ends of the Rear Wheel Pin, take the two Rear Wheel Pin Covers and push tabs 72 and 73 into slots 72 and 73 on the Left Swinging Arm.

Then insert tabs 74 and 75 into slots 74 and 75 on the Right Swinging Arm.

49. Make up the Front Wheel in the same way as the Back Wheel. Take the piece numbered 76 (the Front Wheel Pin) and form a square-sided tube by folding in all the scored edges.

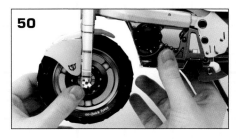

50. To connect the Front Wheel to the Front Forks place the wheel between the two forks and push the Front Wheel Pin through all three holes. Open up the ends to secure.

51. Place the Front Wheel Pin Covers over the ends of the pin by placing tabs 77, 78, 79 and 80 into their respective slots, as you did with the Back Wheel.

52. Fix the Instrument Panel onto the motorcycle by pushing tab 81 into slot 81 on the Screen.

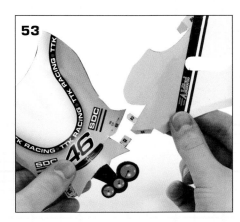

53. Take the Right Side Panel and fix it to the Screen by pushing tabs 82 and 83 into their respective slots.

Remember to open up the small tabs once the tab is through the slot to secure.

54. Take the Left Side Panel and fix it to the Screen by pushing tabs 84 and 85 into their respective slots.

55. Take the Bottom Faring piece and fix it to the Left Side Panel by pushing tab 86 into slot 86.

Pushing tab 87 into slot 87 will fix the Bottom Faring to the Right Side Panel.

56. To attach the levers to the handlebars, push tab 88 on the Right Lever into slot 88 on the handlebars.

Push tab 89 on the Left Lever into slot 89 on the handlebars.

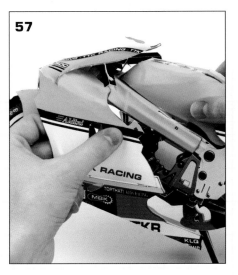

57. To attach the faring onto the motorcycle, from the front of the motorcycle, push the faring whilst feeding the front wheel through the large space in the middle of the faring. Once pushed up, push tabs 90 and 91 on the side panels into their respective slots.

58. The foot rests slot into place by pushing the small tabs into the slots on the Rear Frame.

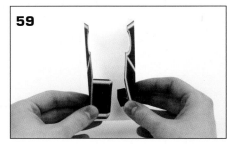

59. To complete the stand for your model, simply push tab 92 into slot 92.

Congratulations!
You have completed your model.

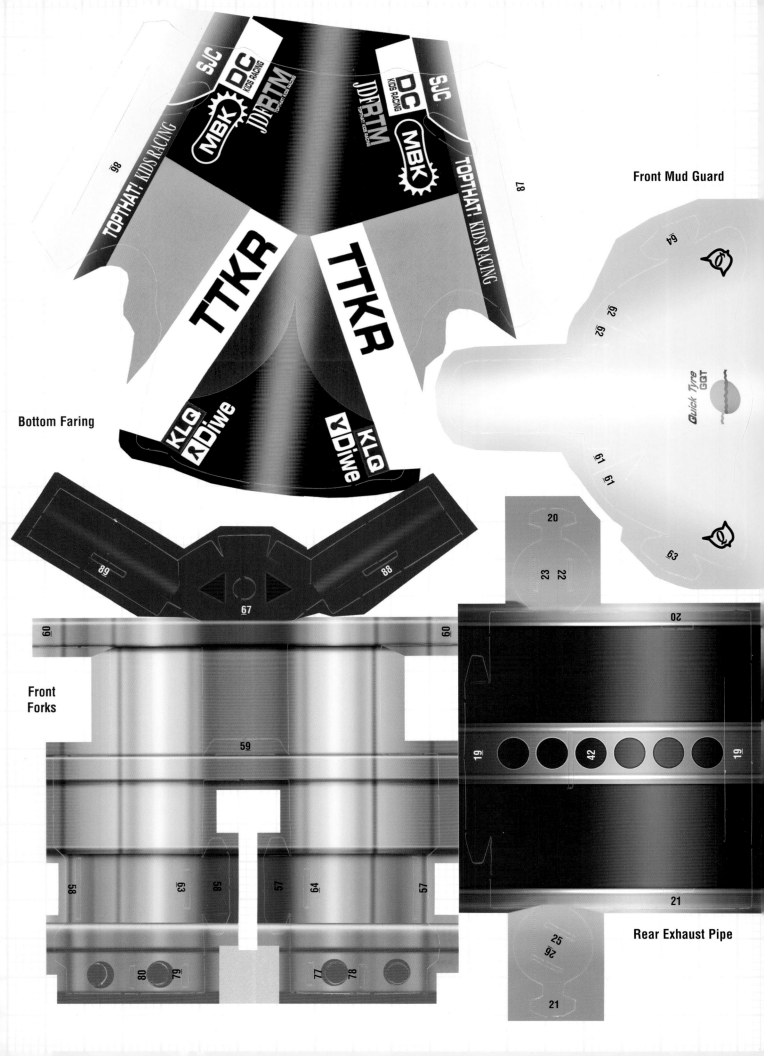

Front Mud Guard

Bottom Faring

Front Forks

Rear Exhaust Pipe

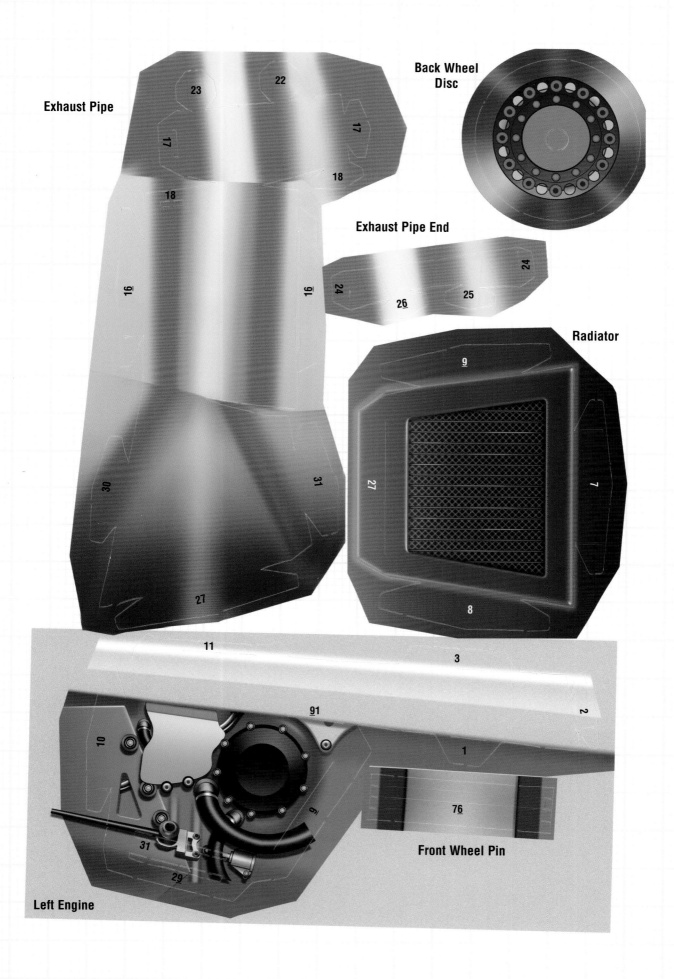

Exhaust Pipe

Back Wheel Disc

Exhaust Pipe End

Radiator

Left Engine

Front Wheel Pin

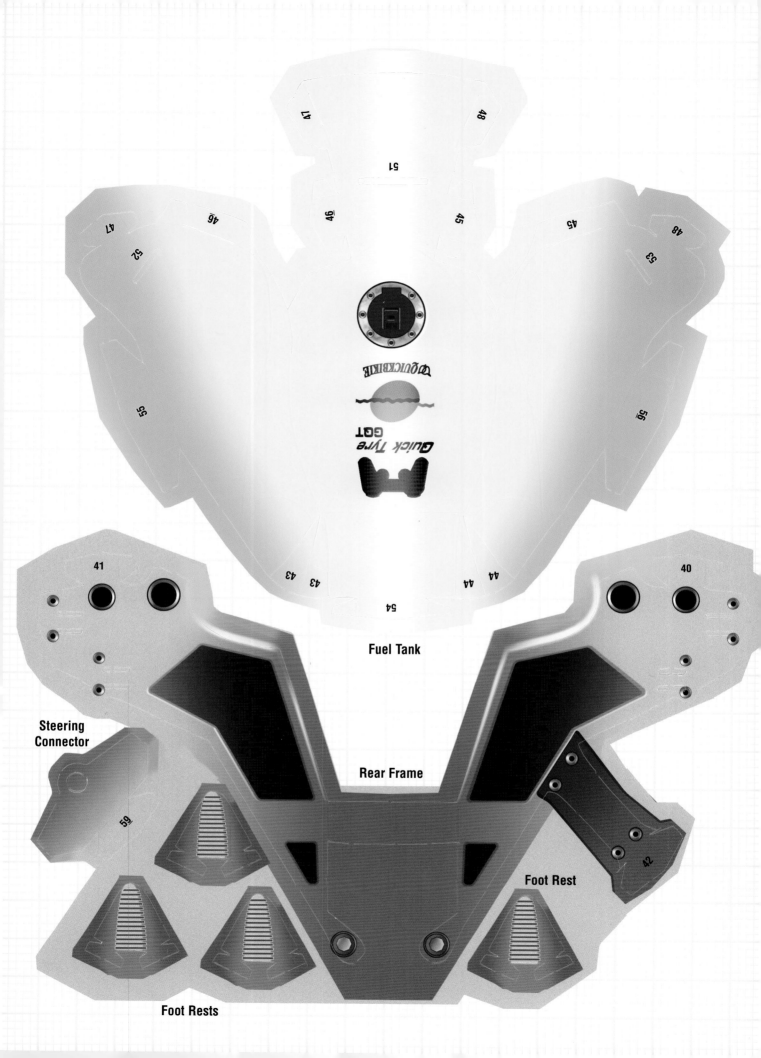

Fuel Tank

Steering
Connector

Rear Frame

Foot Rest

Foot Rests

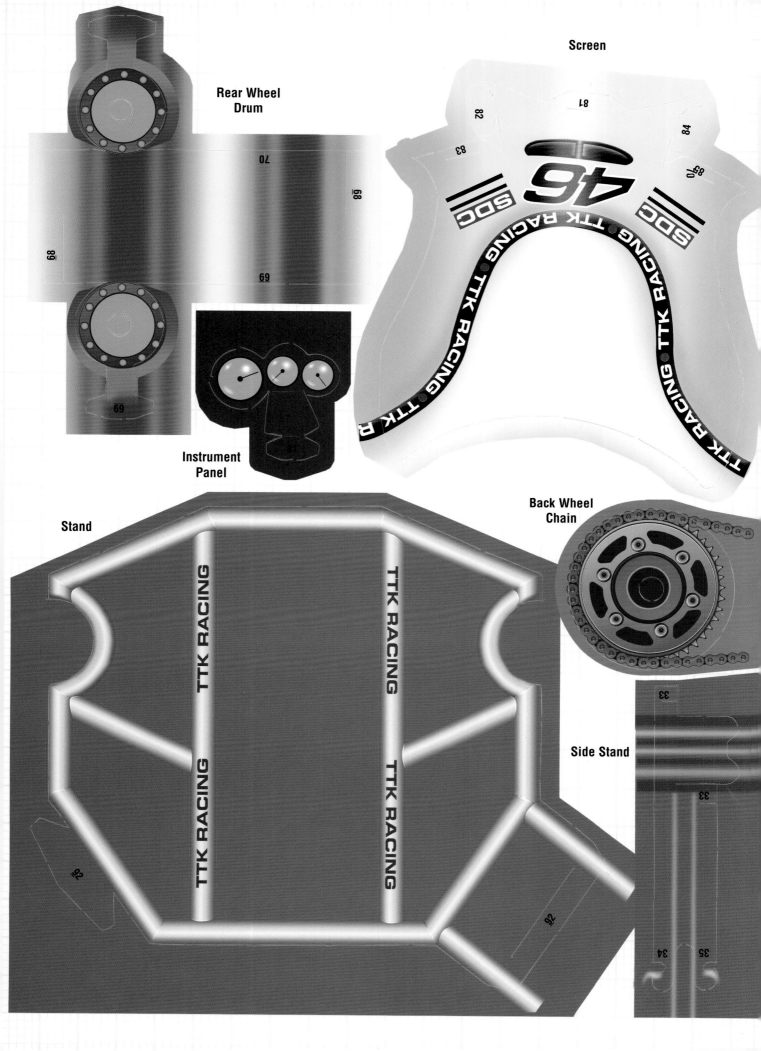

Rear Wheel Drum

Screen

Instrument Panel

Stand

Back Wheel Chain

Side Stand

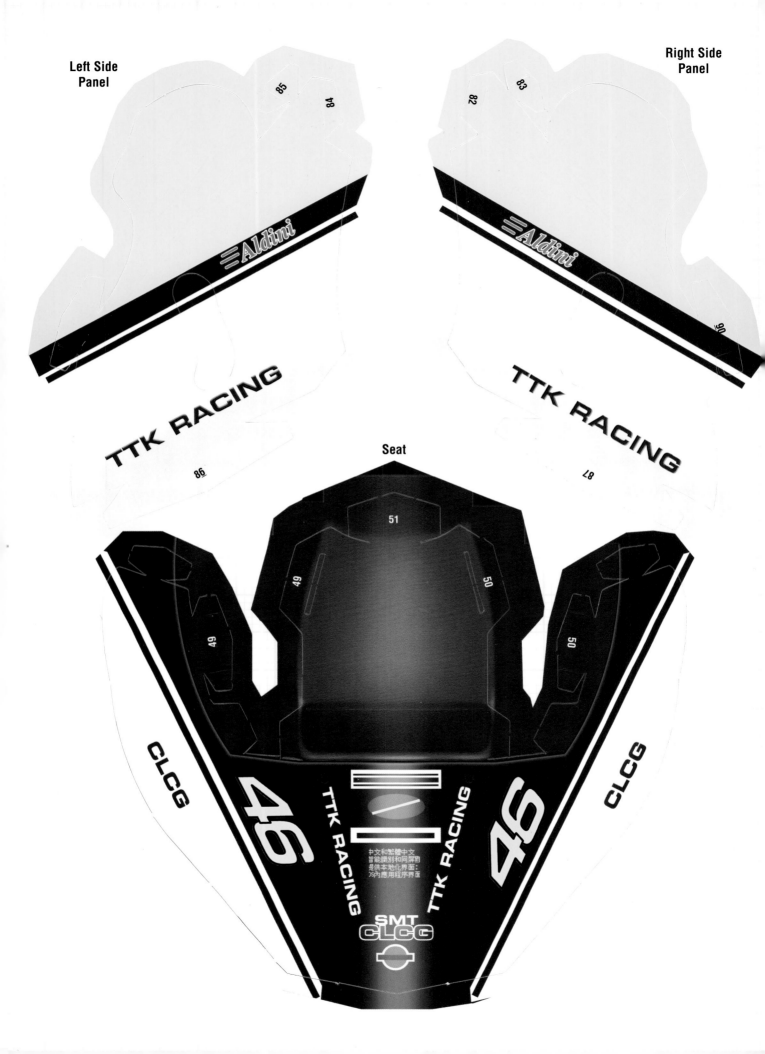

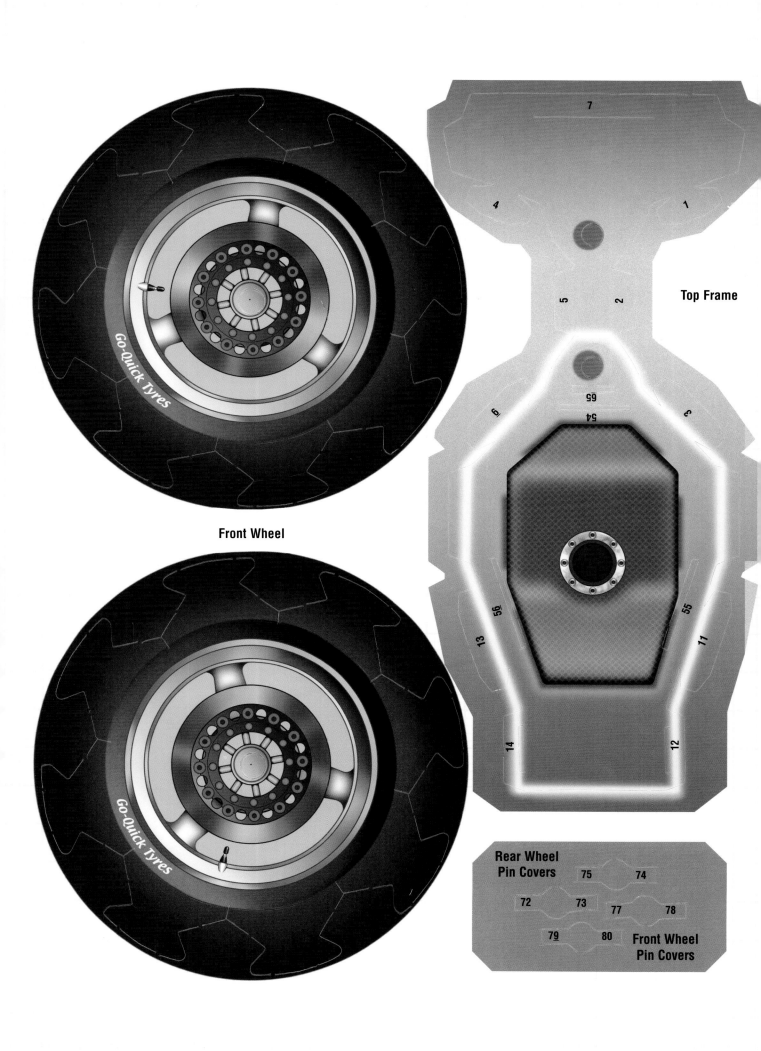

Front Wheel

Top Frame

Rear Wheel Pin Covers

Front Wheel Pin Covers

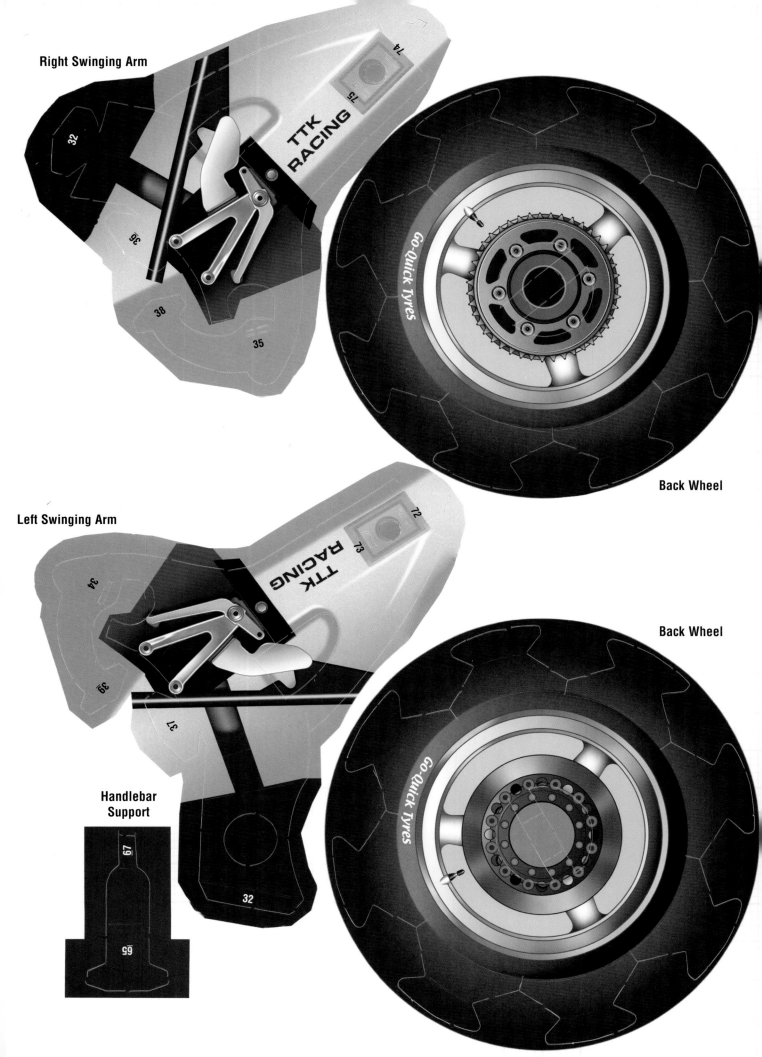

Right Swinging Arm

32

36

38

35

TTK RACING

74

75

Back Wheel

Go-Quick Tyres

Left Swinging Arm

34

39

37

72

73

TTK RACING

Back Wheel

Go-Quick Tyres

Handlebar Support

67

65

32

PRESS OUT AND BUILD
APACHE HELICOPTER

THE FLYING TANK

The Apache is possibly the most impressive military helicopter on active service in the world today. Since it was introduced it has played a decisive part in many military actions.

Why is the Apache so special?

With its arrival, the Apache revolutionised the way in which warfare is conducted. Unlike the helicopters that had come before, the Apache is designed to survive heavy attack and inflict massive damage on ground forces.

Using its radar systems, night vision and sensor systems the Apache can find specific targets day and night, whatever the weather. When targets have been located, the Apache's terrific firepower makes it a formidable threat to ground forces.

How does the Apache work?

The Apache works in the same way as most helicopters. Two rotors spin several blades – these are tilted aerofoils that work in the same way as an aeroplane wing. As the rotor speeds up and the aerofoils go faster the helicopter begins to lift off the ground. In the case of the Apache, the blades are each 6 metres (20 ft) long. The pilot manoeuvres the helicopter by adjusting the swash plate mechanism. The

The Apache can fly low with great accuracy.

controls are very sophisticated, enabling the pilot to keep the helicopter stable.

The automatic flight control system includes instruments like automatic hover hold. This means that the Apache can comfortably hover at a particular height and fly low with great

precision. If the pilot tilts each blade equally, the helicopter can be lifted straight up and down. To move in a particular direction, the pilot simply changes the angle at which the blades tilt as they rotate.

The force with which the main rotor spins acts on the whole helicopter so that the tail could start to swing round also. To stop this happening, there are smaller rotor blades on the tail of the helicopter. These push the tail in the opposite direction.

If the pilot wants to rotate the helicopter in a particular direction, they can change the

ATTACK HELICOPTER
The Apache is a twin-engined army attack helicopter which first entered service with the US Army in 1984.

angle at which the rear blades are tilted.

On the Apache, there are two tail rotors and these have two blades. The tail rotors are designed to allow the Apache to move with greater agility than other helicopters.

How are the Apache's blades made?

Due to the way it is used in military situations, the Apache's blades need to be extremely tough. The helicopter often flies very low – this is called 'nap of the earth' flying. This means there is a danger the Apache could hit trees or buildings.

To make certain that, if this happens, the Apache will not go down, it has particularly tough blades.

Each blade is made up of five arms built out of glass-fibre tubes covered with stainless steel. The edge of the blade that is most likely to hit an object is covered with very tough titanium.

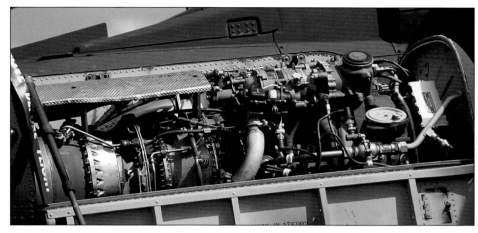

The latest Apaches have turboshaft engines.

How powerful is the Apache's engine?

The latest Apache, the AH-64D has two General Electric T700-GE-701C turboshaft engines. Each engine is mounted on either side of the fuselage of the helicopter.

MANOEUVRING
To change direction, the pilot adjusts a gadget called the swash plate mechanism. This gives the blades uneven lift and tilts the helicopter in the direction the pilot wants to go.

Flying the Apache

As with any helicopter, the pilot uses collective and cyclic controls. There are three display panels which provide the pilot with incredibly sophisticated navigation and flight information.

The display panels are digital, making them much easier to read than traditional dials. All the pilot has to do is press buttons on the side of the display for the necessary information to be revealed.

The Apache's blades are particularly tough.

THE COCKPIT

The Apache's cockpit is divided into sections with the co-pilot gunner in front and the pilot behind on an elevated seat.

Inside the Apache cockpit.

sides of the cockpit, as well as the area between the crew cockpits, are protected by lightweight armour shields.

Although parts surrounding the cockpit are designed to crumple on impact, the cockpit itself is very rigid. Both the seats and helicopter structure are intended to give the crew a 95% chance of surviving an impact of up to 12.8 metres a second.

To protect the pilot and co-pilot gunner against fire from beneath, the seats are made of a bullet-proof material, called Kevlar®.

Between the two cockpits there is a transparent blast barrier, which is designed to give the best possible vision. The floor and

RPM
The Apache's 30 mm automatic cannon can fire 625 rounds of ammunition in one minute. The gun is located under the fuselage.

The Longbow Apache.

Apaches are designed to destroy heavily armoured ground targets like tanks and bunkers. This means that the helicopter needs to have real firepower as well as an excellent targeting system.

Apaches are armed with the lethal Hellfire missile.

The Hellfire missile is the Apache's main weapon and is more than up to the job of taking out enemy targets. For close range targeting, the Apache has a Boeing M230 Chain Gun 30 mm automatic cannon.

Usually, the co-pilot gunner is responsible for firing both the missiles and the gun. The pilot can, however, override his copilot's controls to fire the gun and launch missiles.

When a Hellfire missile hits its target, an impact sensor sets off the warhead.

APACHE HELICOPTER

The radar dome sits on top of the mast.

How does the Apache find its targets?

Apache helicopters have the most remarkable sensor equipment for finding targets.

In the latest Apaches, a radar dome which uses radio waves for detection is mounted on the mast. It rotates 360 degrees and can detect up to 256 targets at any one time.

Objects such as tanks, trucks and other aircraft, once they're spotted, are compared to a database of shapes. The crew can then tell what they're looking at. Targets are pinpointed using the Apache's display panels.

For night operations, the crew uses night vision sensors which are attached to a turret under the nose of the craft. These sensors detect the infrared light given off by heated objects. During the daytime, a normal video camera and telescope are used. Whether the crew are using night vision or video, the images are sent to a small display in each crew member's helmet. The image is also sent to a lens in front of their right eye.

Infrared sensors in the cockpit translate how the pilot positions their helmet and send the information to the turret. This means that pilots can actually aim the sensors just by moving their head.

The Apache can destroy heavily armoured tanks.

How does the Apache avoid trouble?

Flying any helicopter in a war situation is obviously dangerous but, the Apache has very sophisticated evasion systems.

By reducing its own infrared signature, the Apache can evade heat-seeking missiles. The most recent Apaches also have an infrared jammer that generates infrared energy at different levels to confuse heat-seeking missiles.

What would it cost to buy an Apache?

To buy one of the new Longbow Apache helicopters would cost £12 million. The basic AH-64A Apache costs £9.3 million and the additional modifications cost £2.6 million.

HELICOPTER HISTORY

As with so many things – including gunpowder – it seems as though the Chinese were the first to explore the basic idea of helicopter-type flight. Chinese children played with a hand-spun toy called a 'flying top' that rose straight up in the air as it revolved rapidly.

Leonardo da Vinci, the famous artist and inventor, was probably the first person to imagine a helicopter powerful enough to lift a human being.

In around 1500, da Vinci made drawings of a machine that used muscular power to turn the helicopter's rotor. Da Vinci's design would have worked in theory but there would have been no way that muscle power would have been enough to drive the machine.

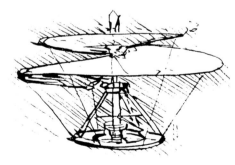

An early helicopter design by da Vinci.

Da Vinci's basic problems also troubled inventors who followed him: how to lift the helicopter off the ground and how to invent an engine that was powerful enough.

One of the first helicopters, designed by Spaniard Raoul Pescara.

The breakthrough

The internal combustion engine was invented at the end of the nineteenth century. It was only then that it became possible for the pioneers of helicopter flight to develop full-sized models equipped with the necessary power.

In the first part of the twentieth century, pioneers across the world began the race to build a helicopter that would fly using an internal combustion engine.

Among them were the Frenchman Maurice Leger, Raoul Pescara in Spain, Emile Berliner and his son Henry in the USA and the Russian, Igor I Sikorsky.

When these pioneers began experimenting, they hit the fundamental problem of how to stop the rotor from rotating the whole helicopter in the opposite direction to the engine.

This problem was solved by the invention of the swash plate. The swash plate allows rotor blade angles to be altered to make the helicopter's lift equal on both sides of the central shaft.

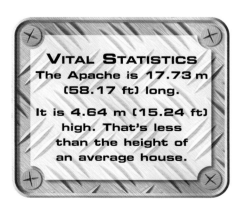

VITAL STATISTICS
The Apache is 17.73 m (58.17 ft) long.

It is 4.64 m (15.24 ft) high. That's less than the height of an average house.

HELICOPTERS TODAY

Today, helicopters are used extensively in cities and for shorter flights carrying between one and fifty people. They have two main advantages over other aircraft – they can fly slowly or hover and take off and land in restricted spaces.

COMBAT RANGE
The Apache has a combat range of 482 km (300 miles)

A helicopter arriving at a city landing pad.

In cities, the versatility and manoeuvrability of helicopters make them perfect for aerial coverage of news events. Television audiences have become used to images of high-speed car chases and other dramatic events broadcast live to studios from helicopters.

Helicopters are also used to make traffic reports for television and radio stations.

As a status symbol for business people, helicopters have come into their own. They're ideal for today's busy executive who needs to get from meeting to meeting quickly. The emergence of city airports and landing pads on roofs has also made this possible.

Land and sea rescue and other non-military uses

The helicopter's superior manoeuvrability means it can help rescue a person caught in the sea or on a mountain ledge, or in other hazardous places. If it's not possible to land, a helicopter can hover to rescue people while a rope ladder is lowered.

Helicopters are often used to rescue people from danger.

SPEED
The Apache has a cruising speed of 233 km/h (145 mph) and a maximum speed of 261 km/h (162 mph).

Once recovered, people can be transported to hospital quickly and safely.

Helicopters have proved particularly valuable to the offshore oil and gas industry, transporting people and supplies. Their ability to hover and fly slowly makes helicopters invaluable for inspecting pipelines from the air.

Other uses include fire patrols, crop dusting with insecticides and the aerial planting of seeds for reforestation and erosion control.

Helicopter firefighters.

OTHER HELICOPTERS

The Boeing CH-47 Chinook.

The Boeing CH-47 Chinook

The Chinook is one of the great workhorse cargo-carrying helicopters. It is a twin-engined, tandem rotor helicopter designed to transport ammunition, personnel and supplies. Today, though, the Chinook is also used for rescue and transporting people and heavy equipment.

Chinooks were first developed in the early 1950s and the CH-47 Series Chinook began production in 1956. It has been consistently developed and improved since then.

How much a Chinook can carry depends on the model, the nature of its cargo, how far it has to fly and the weather conditions.

A S-70A Black Hawk helicopter.

The S-70A Black Hawk multi-mission helicopter

Developed by the Sikorsky Aircraft Corporation, the Black Hawk has been operational in the US army since 1976.

Black Hawk helicopters were developed as troop carriers – carrying up to eleven fully-equipped troops – and logistical support aircraft. They can also be adapted to carry out medical evacuation, command-and-control, search and rescue, armed escort, electronic warfare and for executive transport.

Key features of Black Hawk

CH-47 CHINOOK
This is an unusual helicopter in that it has three rotors at the front and three rotors at the rear.

helicopters include their ability to avoid detection and their remarkable manoeuvrability when flying close to the ground. They can carry sixteen Hellfire missiles as well as, if necessary, rockets, cannons and electronic countermeasure pods.

Since they were introduced, Black Hawks have logged four million flying hours. They've seen action in Grenada, Panama, Kuwait, Somalia and have taken part in rescue missions and humanitarian actions, including in Bosnia.

A S-70A Black Hawk Hospital helicopter.

BLACK HAWK
The Black Hawk S-70A can be armed with a variety of missiles, rockets, machine guns and a 20 mm cannon.

ASSEMBLY INSTRUCTIONS

The Apache helicopter is put together in numbered order: starting with 1, moving to 2 and so on. All dotted lines indicate scored edges which are to be folded. Adult help may be required.

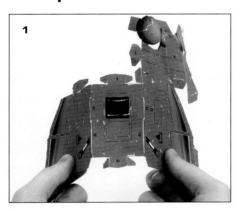

1. Holding the Cockpit piece face up, bend down all the scored edges.

4. Pull the Nose piece backwards to fit tab 4 into slot 4. Make sure that the tabs are concealed inside the Nose piece as you put it together. You will always need to pull out the smaller tabs on each tab once it is through the slot to secure it in place.

EXPENSIVE
Apache helicopters are very expensive, with each one costing many millions of pounds to build.

2. Taking the two slots numbered 1, pull them together until they easily slot into each other to form a small cone shape. Repeat with the slots numbered 2.

5. Repeat with tab and slot 5. Tab and slot 6 pull the base of the cockpit together and lock it in place.

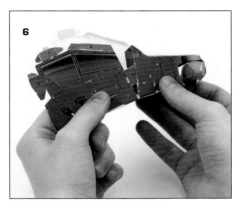

6. Tab 7 pushes into slot 7 to pull the left side of the Cockpit into place.

3. To fix the Nose piece onto the Cockpit, push tab 3 into slot 3.

LETHAL WEAPON
Many people believe that the Apache Longbow is the most advanced aerial fighting vehicle in the world.

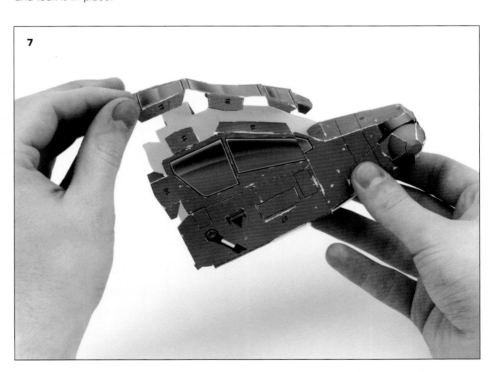

7. Take the Windscreen piece and hold it face up. Bend down all the scored edges to make it flexible. To attach the Windscreen to the Cockpit push tabs 8 to 12 into their respective slots, remembering to open up the smaller tabs to secure, once the tabs are through the slots.

LOW FLIER
The Apache is designed to fly low to the ground. This helps it to hide behind cover such as trees.

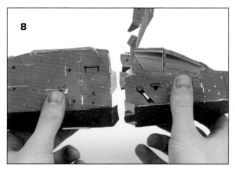

8. Hold the Mid Section face up and bend down all the scored edges. To attach the Mid Section to the Cockpit, push tab 13 into slot 13 remembering to secure it in place by opening up the small tabs once through the slot. Push tabs 14 and 15 through their respective slots to close up the Mid Section.

9. To close up the helicopter's roof, push tabs 16 and 17 into slots 16 and 17. Make sure that all roof tabs are neatly tucked in as you pull it into place. Tabs 18 and 19 push into their respective slots to complete the roof of the helicopter.

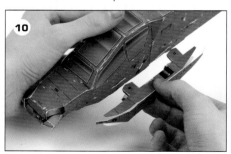

10. To fix the Right Section to the helicopter, push tabs 20 to 23 into slots 20 to 23 on the Cockpit and Mid Section. Once this is in place secure it further by pushing the end tabs numbered 24 and 25 into their respective slots.

11. This process is repeated to fix the Left Section to the helicopter. Push tabs 26 to 29 into the slots 26 to 29 on the Cockpit and Mid Section. Once this is in place, again secure it further by pushing the end tabs numbered 30 to 31 into their respective slots.

12. Take the Right Engine Filter and bend down all the scored edges to make it flexible.

13. Push tab 32 into slot 32 and tab 33 into slot 33. This bit may be tricky so you will need to be patient whilst making this small part.

14. Attach the Right Engine Filter to the Right Engine by pushing tab 34 through slot 34.

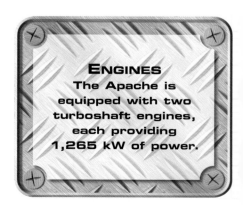

ENGINES
The Apache is equipped with two turboshaft engines, each providing 1,265 kW of power.

15. Tab and slot 35 will secure the filter in place at the front of the engine.

16. Next you will need to attach the Right Engine onto the Mid Section of the helicopter. To do this push tabs 36 to 39 through slots 36 to 39. Remember to open up the small tabs once through the slots to secure it. Once this is in place, you may need to shape it carefully if you have squashed any pieces. Ensure all tabs are tucked inwards as these pieces are attached to each other.

17. Take the Left Engine Filter and bend down all the scored edges to make it flexible.

ENGINE PROTECTION
The engines are mounted above the fins on either side of the fuselage. They are armour-protected.

18. Push tab 40 into slot 40 and tab 41 into slot 41. This bit may be tricky so you will need to be patient whilst making this small part.

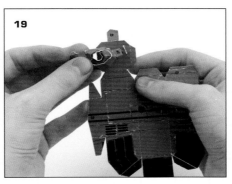

19. Attach the Left Engine Filter to the Left Engine by pushing tab 42 through slot 42.

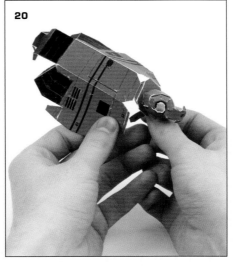

20. Tab and slot 43 will secure the filter in place at the front of the engine.

21. Next you will need to attach the Left Engine onto the Mid Section of the helicopter. To do this push tabs 44 to 47 through slots 44 to 47. Again, once this is in place, you may need to shape it carefully if you have squashed any pieces. Make sure all tabs are tucked neatly inside.

22. To make the tail of the helicopter, take the Middle Tail Section and Bottom Tail Section and fold down all scored edges. The Bottom Tail Section needs to be bent around to form a smooth curved shape. Push tabs 48 to 53 into their respective slots to complete the tail. This bit may need a little patience. Remember to open up the small tabs once the tabs are through the slots.

23. Make the Top Tail Section by holding it face up and bending down all the scored edges. Fix it onto the Middle Tail Section by pushing tabs 54 to 57 into their respective slots.

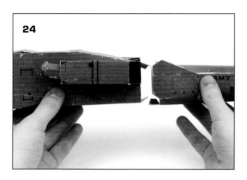

24. The helicopter tail is now joined onto the Mid Section. Push tabs 58 and 59 into slots 58 and 59 to do this.

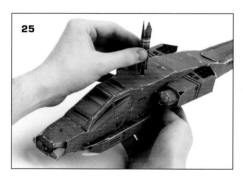

25. Make up the Rotor Pin by bending all the scored edges and wrapping it around to form a square-shaped tube. Push tabs 60 and 61 into slots 60 and 61 on the top of the helicopter.

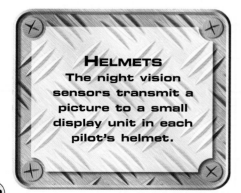

HELMETS
The night vision sensors transmit a picture to a small display unit in each pilot's helmet.

26. Make up the Rotor Pin Support by bending down all the scored edges. Attach it to the top of the helicopter by pushing the Rotor Pin through the hole in the middle. Secure in place by pushing tabs 62, 63 and 64 into their respective slots.

Night Vision
Both the pilot and the gunner can use night vision sensors. These sensors are attached to the Apache's nose.

27. Take the Right Missile Support and bend down all the scored edges. Attach it to the Right Missile Launcher by pushing tabs 65 and 66 into their respective slots.

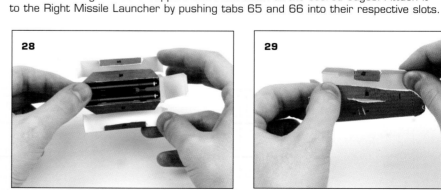

28. To complete the Right Missile Launcher, fold in the sides, making sure the tabs tuck in neatly, and push tabs 67 and 68 into their respective slots to form a box shape.

29. To make the Right Wing, bend down all the scored edges to make it flexible. Fold it over on itself and secure it by pushing tab 69 into slot 69.

30. Attach the Right Missile Launcher to the Right Wing by pushing tabs 70 and 71 into slots 70 and 71.

33. To complete the Left Missile Launcher, fold in the sides making sure the tabs tuck in neatly and push tabs 76 and 77 into their respective slots to form a box shape.

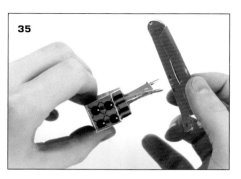

35. Attach the Left Missile Launcher to the Left Wing by pushing tabs 79 and 80 into slots 79 and 80.

31. To attach this whole assembly to the body, push tabs 72 and 73 into slot 72 and 73. This is a bit tricky so be patient.

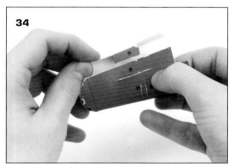

34. To make the Left Wing, bend down all the scored edges to make it flexible. Fold it over on itself and secure it by pushing tab 78 into slot 78.

36. To attach this whole assembly to the body, push tabs 81 and 82 into slots 81 and 82.

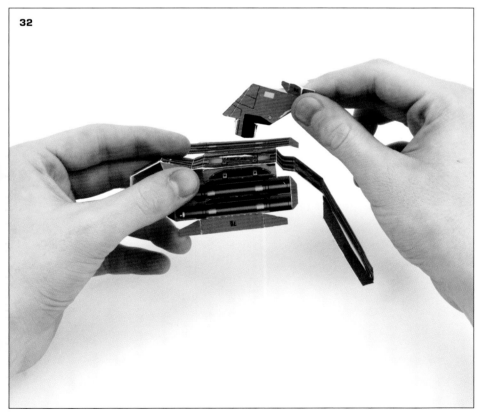

37. Push tab 83 into slot 83 to secure the end of the tail section of the helicopter.

MILITARY PURPOSE
The main purpose of the Apache is to destroy heavily protected ground targets.

32. Take the Left Missile Support and bend down all the scored edges. Attach it to the Left Missile Launcher by pushing tabs 74 and 75 into their respective slots.

38. Form the Rear Wheel by folding down the scored edges and folding it in half. Push tabs 84 into the slot numbered 84 to attach it to the tail of the helicopter.

39. Make the Gun by folding down the scored edges and bending it around to form a three-sided tube. Take the Gun Support and bend its scored edges down too. Tuck it around and hold the bottom tabs together whilst you push on the Gun. This is done by pushing the slots numbered 85 on the Gun onto the tab you are holding.

40. Fix this whole assembly onto your helicopter by pushing tabs 86 and 87 into their respective slots on the underneath of the helicopter.

41. Take the Tail Fin piece and bend down all the scored edges to make it flexible. Fold it in half and tuck tab 88 into slot 88 to secure it.

42. To form a support for the rear rotor, tuck tab 89 into slot 89.

43. Then bend the two long tabs around and tuck them in to complete the curved shape of the rotor support.

HELLFIRE
The Apache carries Hellfire missiles. These are powerful enough to burn through the thickest tank armour.

SERVICE RECORD
The US Army has more than 800 Apaches in service.

44. To attach the Rear Rotor, fold down all the scored edges and then push the two tabs numbered 90 into the hole numbered 90 on the top of the Tail Fin.

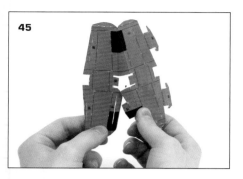

45. Make up the Tail Wing by pushing down all the scored edges to make it flexible.

46. Push tab 91 into slot 91 then fold it over on itself and push tabs 92 and 93 into their respective slots.

47. Take the Tail Fin and push tabs 94 and 95 into slots 94 and 95 on the top of the helicopter's tail to fix it in place.

48. Take the Tail Wing and push slots 96 into slots 96 at the rear of the Tail Fin to attach it. This completes the rear end of the helicopter.

49. Push down all the scored edges on the Base to make it flexible. Push tab 97 into slot 97 to lock it into shape.

OTHER MISSILES
The helicopter is also equipped with air-to-air missiles, such as Stingers, Sidewinders, Mistrals and Sidearms, and 70 mm rockets.

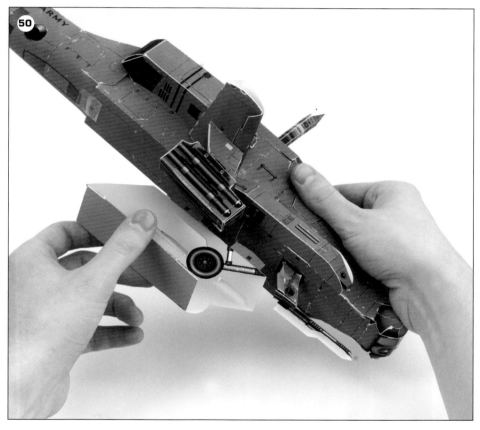

50. Push tabs 98 to 101 into slots 98 to 101 on the bottom of the helicopter.

51. Attach the Sensor, after bending down all the scored edges, by pushing tabs 102 and 103 into slots 102 and 103 on the front end of the helicopter.

52. Push down the Rotor Bearing 1 face down over the Rotor Pin.

53

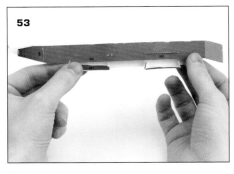

53. Take Rotor Blade 1 and bend down all the scored edges. Fold it over on itself and secure by pushing tabs 104 and 105 into slots 104 and 105.

54

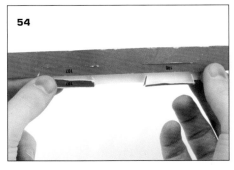

54. Take Rotor Blade 2 and bend down all the scored edges. Fold it over on itself and secure by pushing tabs 106 and 107 into slots 106 and 107.

55

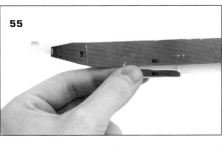

55. Take Rotor Blade 3 and bend down all the scored edges. Fold it over on itself and secure by pushing tabs 108 and 109 into slots 108 and 109.

56

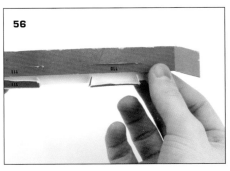

56. Take Rotor Blade 4 and bend down all the scored edges. Fold it over on itself and secure by pushing tabs 110 and 111 into slots 110 and 111.

57

57. Take the Lower Rotor Fixing and bend down all the scored edges before pushing on the rotor blades starting with Rotor Blade 1, tab number 112 into slot 112. Rotor Blade 2 fixes on with tab 113 into slot 113, Rotor Blade 3 attaches by pushing tab 114 into slot 114 and finally, Rotor Blade 4 attaches by pushing tab 115 into slot 115.

58

58. Take the Upper Rotor Fixing and bend down all the scored edges and attach the rotor blades to it by placing tabs 116 to 119 into their respective slots. To make the rotor blades stand firm you will need two pipe cleaners (available in all craft shops). Connect the corresponding blades by inserting the pipe cleaners. Then place the whole rotor assembly onto the Rotor Pin.

59

59. To complete your model place the Rotor Bearing 2 over the Rotor Pin and fix it in place with the Securing Washer.

CONGRATULATIONS!
You have completed your model.

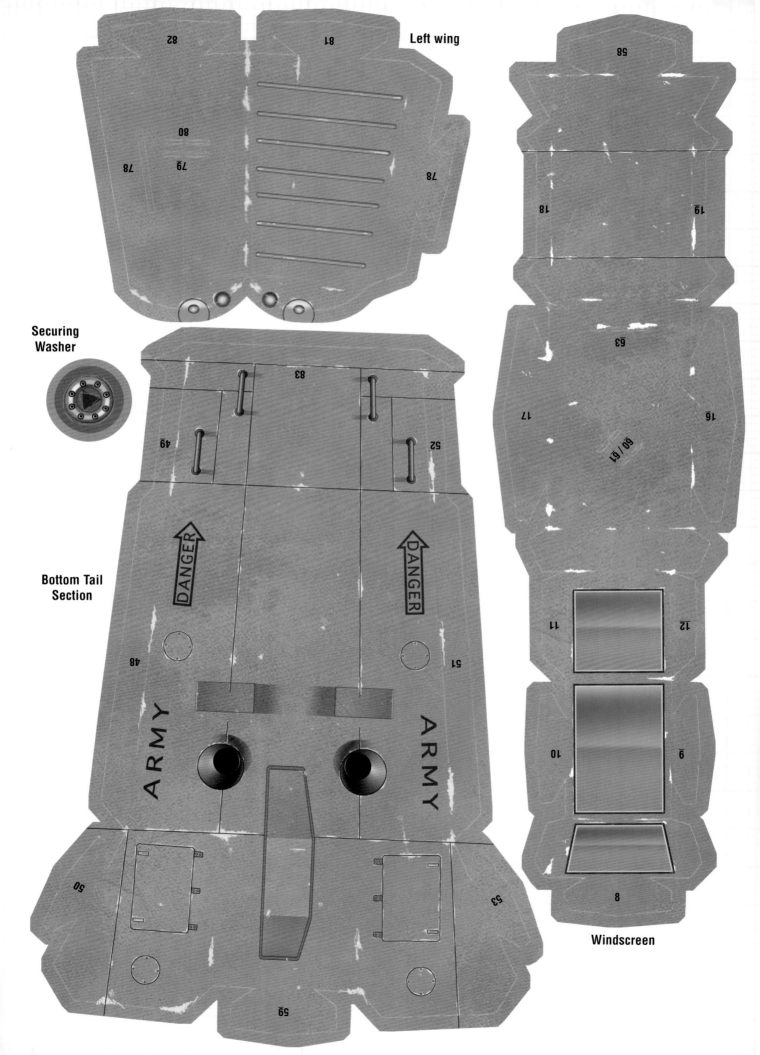

Left wing

Securing
Washer

Bottom Tail
Section

Windscreen

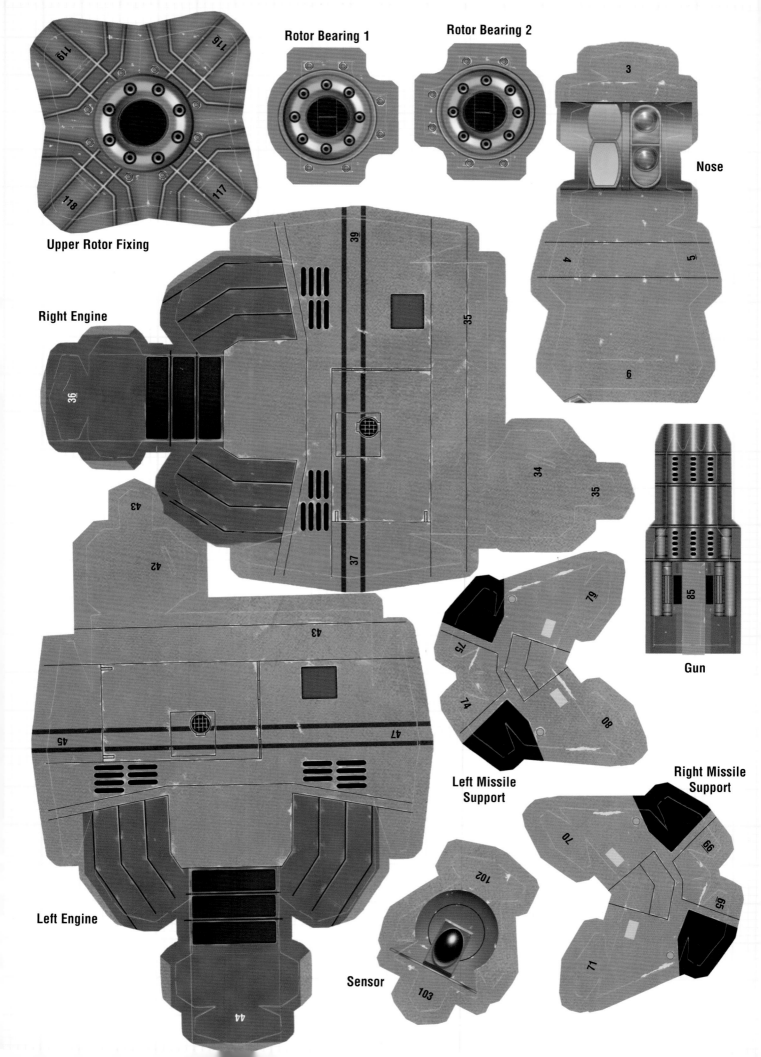

Upper Rotor Fixing

Rotor Bearing 1

Rotor Bearing 2

Nose

Right Engine

Left Engine

Gun

Left Missile Support

Right Missile Support

Sensor

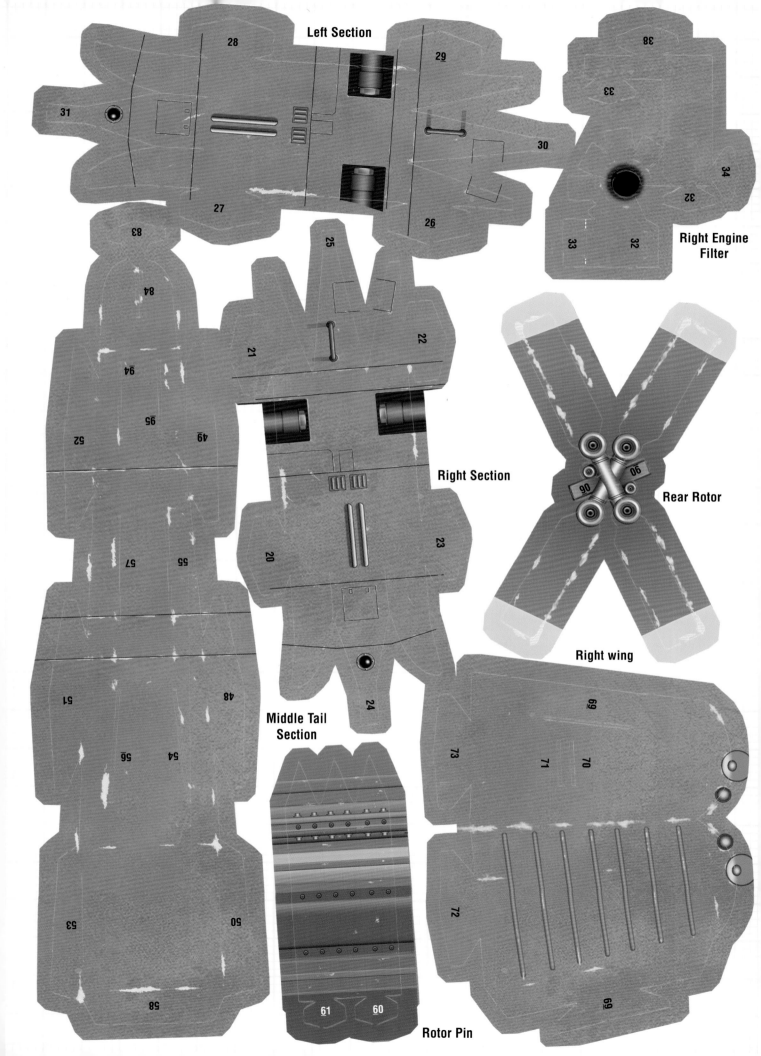

Left Section

28

29

31

30

27

26

Right Engine Filter

38

33

34

32

33   32

83

84

25

94

21

22

95

52   49

Right Section

57   55

20

23

24

Middle Tail Section

51   48

54   56

53   50

58

61   60

Rotor Pin

Rear Rotor

90

90

Right wing

69

73   71   70

72

69

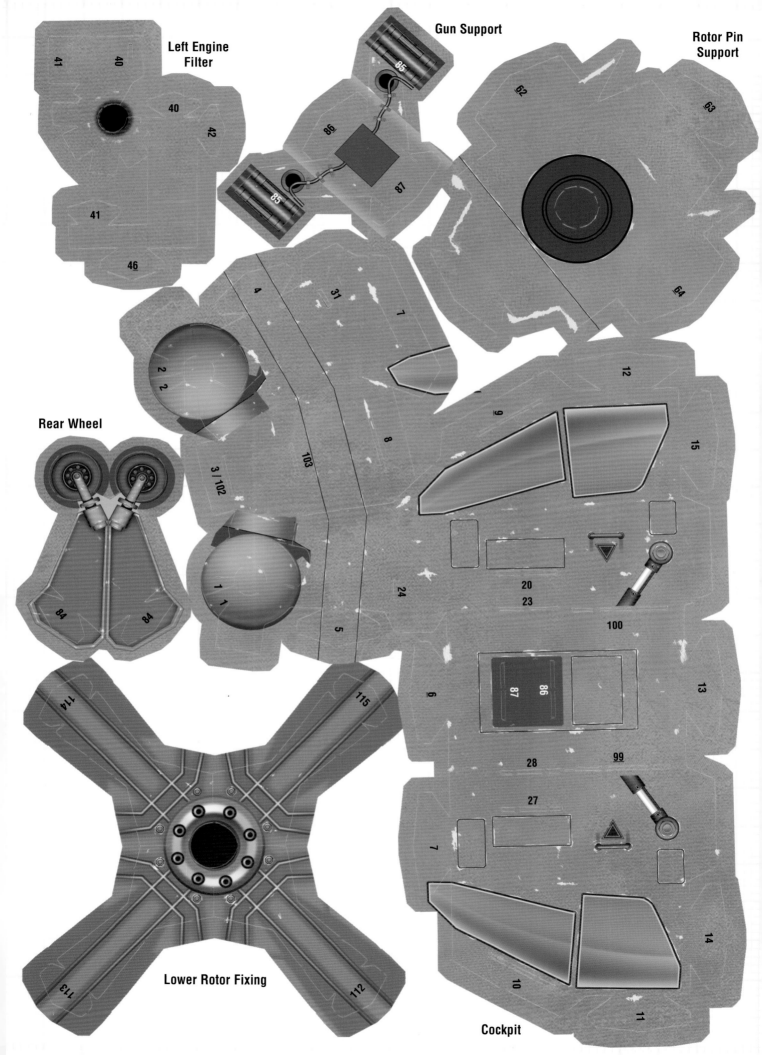

Left Engine
Filter

Gun Support

Rotor Pin
Support

Rear Wheel

Lower Rotor Fixing

Cockpit

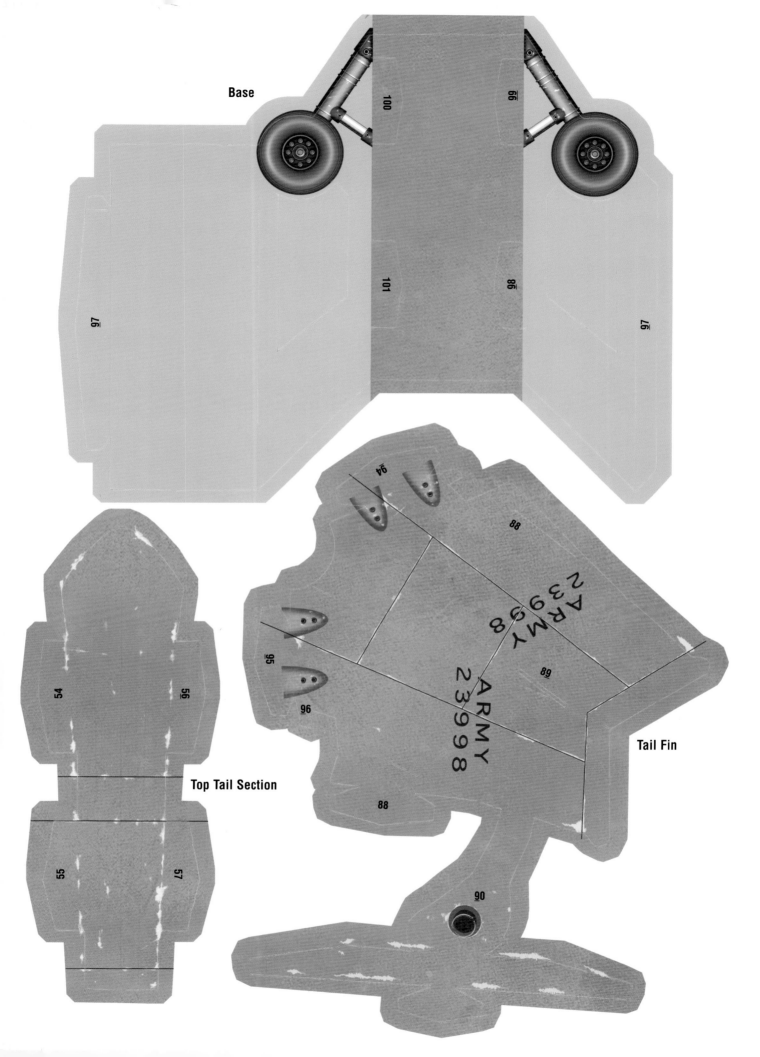

Base

100

99

101

98

67

67

94

88

88

95

96

89

ARMY 23998

90

54

56

55

57

Top Tail Section

Tail Fin

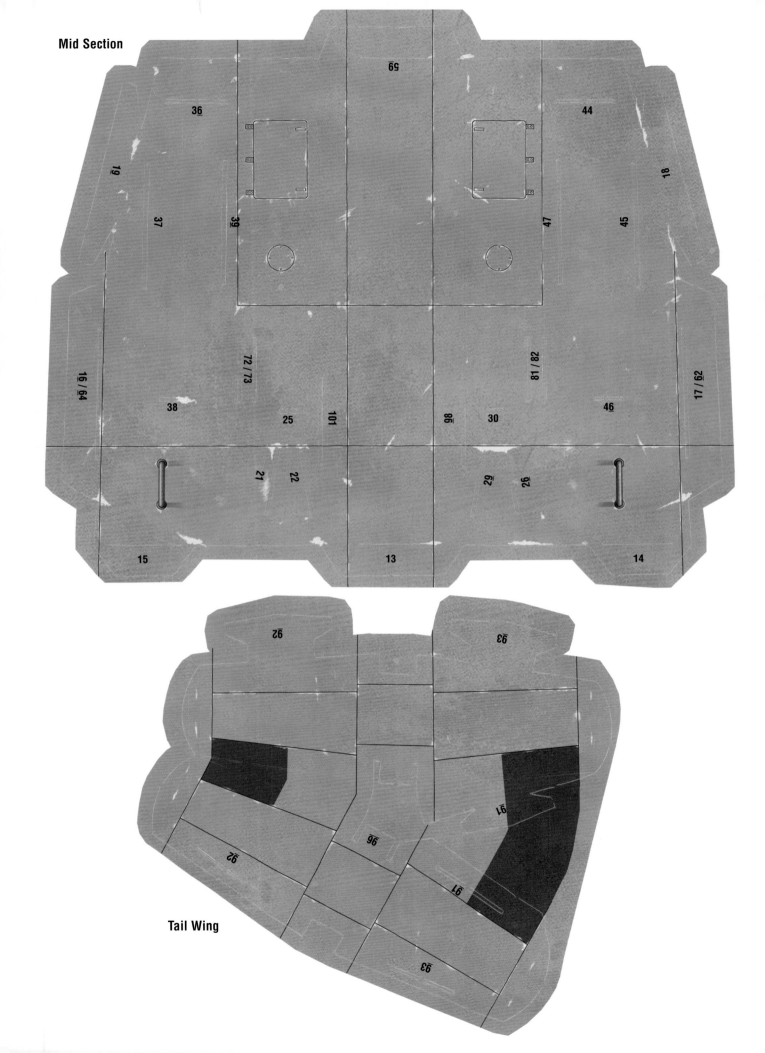

Mid Section

Tail Wing

Rotor Blade 4

Rotor Blade 2

Right Missile Launcher

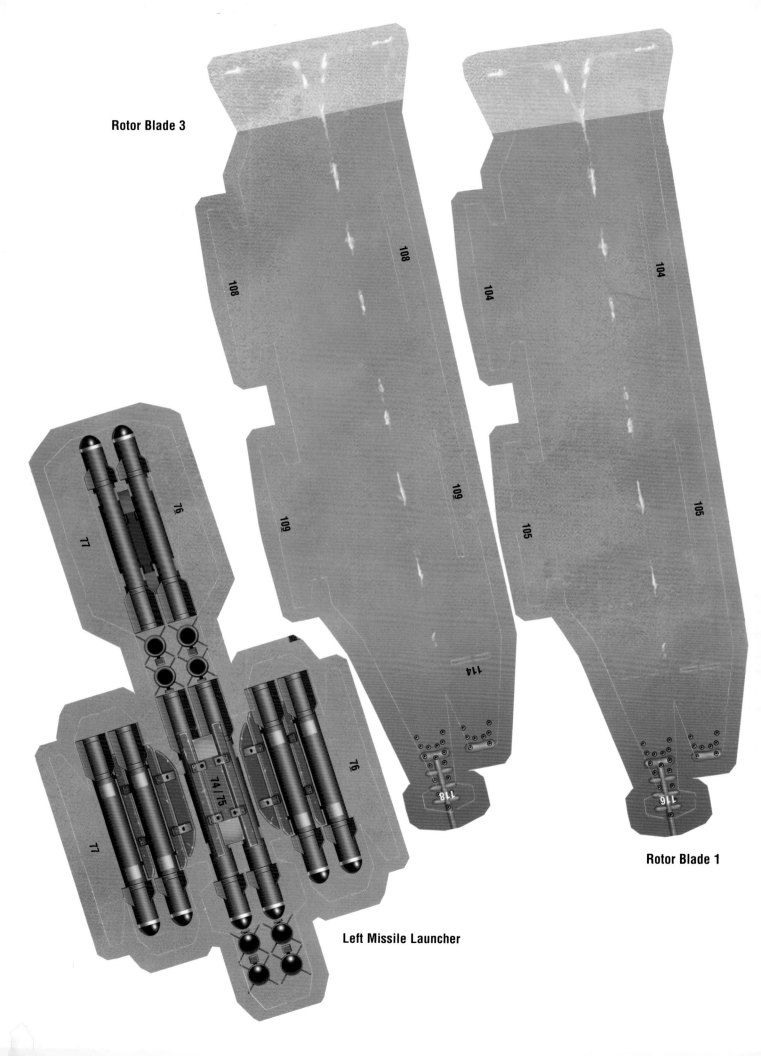

Rotor Blade 3

Left Missile Launcher

Rotor Blade 1

PRESS OUT AND BUILD
RACING CAR

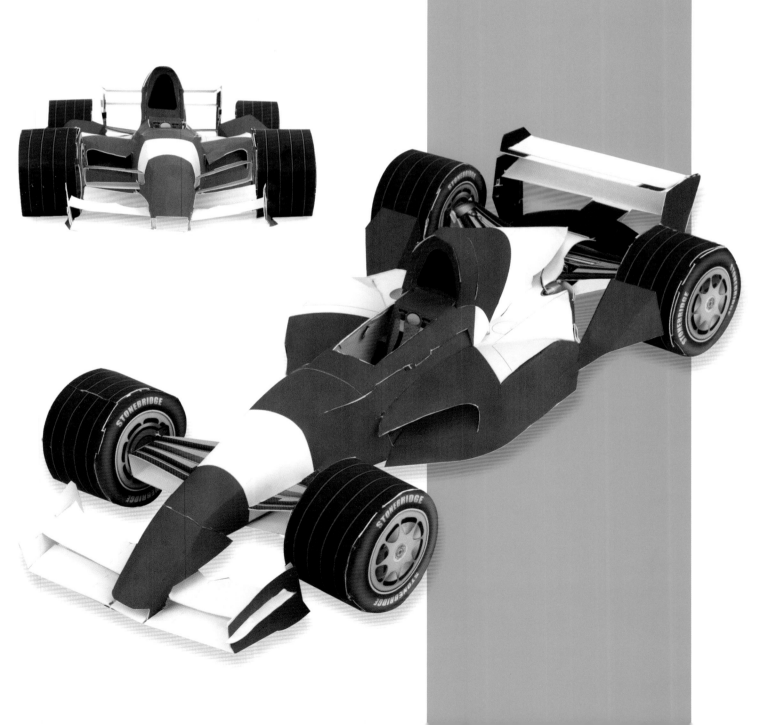

A BRIEF HISTORY OF MOTOR RACING

From Formula One to Indy Car, motor racing attracts millions of viewers and is one of the most popular international sports in the world today!

The first races

The first proper motor race was held in France in 1895. The drivers set off from Paris and raced their cars to Bordeaux. The first driver to finish was Émile Levassor in his Panhard-Levassor. It took him just over 48 hours to cover a distance that would take about seven hours to complete today.

The Bugatti Type 35 from the 1930s.

Closed circuit racing

Closed circuit racing – driving around a circuit and not on the road – developed more quickly in America than it did in Europe. The first race tracks were made from tarred sand or wood. The famous Indianapolis speedway was built in 1909, and the first race was held there in 1911.

Formula One arrives

Formula One (F1) really began after World War II and was originally called Formula A. In 1950, the first British Grand Prix was held at Silverstone – the first officially sanctioned race for Formula One. Racing technology developed at great speed in the 1970s and '80s, and companies spend fortunes developing racing teams today.

Legendary Brazilian F1 racing driver Ayrton Senna in action.

OPTIMUM RACING PERFORMANCE

F1 cars have become increasingly complicated and can race at incredibly high speeds.

Developing technology

The year 1968 saw the introduction of aerofoils or 'wings'. They provide extra downforce, which holds the cars to the track, enabling them to race faster than ever before, particularly around corners.

This 1976 McLaren takes advantage of the downforce provided by its rear aerofoil.

Aerodynamism paved the way for today's cars, which regularly reach speeds of 320 mph (200 kph). To assist the car's aerodynamics, its chassis is built low to the ground. If you look at a modern Formula One car, you'll see that every part of it is built with optimum aerodynamics in mind, from the distinctive nose to the driver's helmet.

During a pit stop highly skilled mechanics refuel the car, change the tyres and repair any minor damage.

Active suspension

In 1987, Team Lotus raced a car with suspension controlled by a computer. Anti-lock brakes and a 'black box', which controlled starting programmes, quickly followed. This type of performance racing car was called an 'active' car and, until racing driver Ayrton Senna was killed in 1994, dominated Formula One. It was after this tragic accident that F1 legislators decided that the cars had become too fast and dangerous. They introduced rules to slow cars down and make it safer for the drivers to race. Although a modern F1 car's suspension cannot be controlled by a computer, it can be minutely adjusted according to track conditions and the type of tyre used.

RACING CAR STATS

Chassis – the monocoque chassis is made from moulded carbon fibre and aluminium honeycomb composite.

Suspension – made from carbon fibre and titanium.

Engine – revs to over 18,000 rpm. It sucks in over 600 litres (130 gallons) of air per second at full speed. The noise it produces reaches 160 decibels, and it uses 75 litres (17 gallons) of fuel per 100 km (62 miles).

Transmission – a six-speed automatic gearbox with one reverse gear.

Fuel system – the risk of fire is reduced by a Kevlar-reinforced rubber fuel cell mounted behind the cockpit.

Cooling system – separate oil and water radiators located on the sides of the car are cooled by air from the car's forward motion.

Cockpit – the removable driver's seat is made from a carbon composite. The gear change and clutch are attached to the steering wheel.

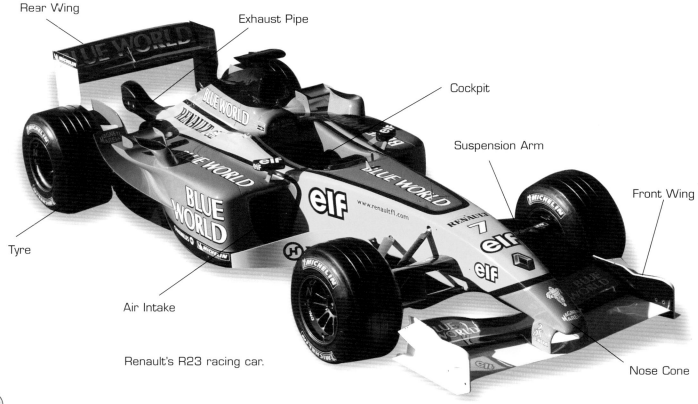

Renault's R23 racing car.

GREAT DRIVERS

Formula One has seen some remarkable drivers. Here are some of the best!

Niki Lauda

Niki Lauda is famous for his skill as a driver. He won two World Championships driving for Ferrari and one with McLaren.

Ayrton Senna

Ayrton Senna was the world's fastest F1 driver in the 1980s and 1990s. He took 65 pole positions – an F1 world record for many years, even after his death at the San Marino Grand Prix in 1994.

Alain Prost

Four times World Champion Alain Prost held the record of most race wins at his retirement, with 51 wins out of 199 races.

Nigel Mansell

Nigel Mansell was known as 'The Lion' due to his fearless driving style. In 1995 he broke the record for the most wins in a single season, winning nine races.

Michael Schumacher

After winning two World Championships back to back for Benetton in 1994 and 1995, Schumacher became the youngest two-time champion in F1 history. But his record-breaking achievements didn't stop there! Schumacher went on to win the World Championship five times for Ferrari, and on his retirement in 2006 he held nearly every record in Formula One, including most pole positions, points scored, fastest laps and race victories.

Lewis Hamilton

Lewis Hamilton took the F1 world by storm at the start of the 2007 season. Despite having never raced an F1 car before, he finished in the top three in each of the first five races and won the sixth, becoming the first driver since Juan Pablo Montoya in 2001 to win a race in his first Formula One season. Lewis then went on to win the World Championship in 2008.

DIFFERENT TYPES OF MOTOR RACING

There are thousands of different motor racing events across the world including sports car racing, stock car racing and extremely challenging motor rallies.

Stock car racing

Stock cars race on a purpose-built track.

Stock car racing originated in America during the 1920s, at a time when alcohol was banned. Gangsters known as bootleggers dealt illegally in alcohol, so they needed fast cars to avoid being caught by the police. Stock car racing was legalised in 1947, and the first official race was held in Daytona in 1948.

Stock cars are modified street cars, with sturdy bodywork able to take the knocks of a fast and furious race. They are sporty and high-tech with plenty of power, and the drivers are protected by a steel cage.

Motor rallies

Rallies feature modified road cars on standard roads and countryside tracks. Races are completed in numerous stages, with the overall best time deciding the winner.

Competitors are usually allowed to drive the course prior to the race, so that they can plan how to tackle the terrain. Co-drivers (or navigators) give a running commentary during the race to describe the route and warn their drivers of potential hazards.

Rally cars are specially adapted to negotiate tricky terrain.

RACING CAR

Drag racing

On the dry lake beds of California in the years after World War II, people began to race their cars over short straight distances without the worry of other drivers or the police. The first 'dragsters' were adapted street cars, with powerful engines and lightweight bodies. Pretty soon, drivers began welding on parts from different cars, exposing the large engines and experimenting with the types of fuel they used, which led to the strictly timed quarter-mile acceleration race known today.

Modern dragsters are incredibly sophisticated, and some are able to accelerate faster than a space shuttle rocket! A top dragster can accelerate from 0–330 mph (530 kph) in 4.5 seconds, and can finish a quarter-mile race in that time! These dragsters go so fast that they have to use parachutes to slow them down once they have finished a race!

Dragsters are designed by computers to have the sleekest profiles, and their wind tunnel-tested aerofoils put enormous pressure on the huge rear wheels, which help to keep them on the ground at high speeds.

The Le Mans 24-hour

Traditionally, drivers of the Le Mans 24-hour race had to make a running start.

Le Mans is one of the oldest and most prestigious races for sports cars. It's officially known as the Le Mans Grand Prix D'Endurance. The original circuit was a huge 60 mile (97 km) triangular course just south of the French city of Le Mans. The first 24-hour race was held in 1923.

Today, the race takes place every June and is held on the Circuit de la Sarthe, which is 8.45 miles (13.6 km) long. Cars race continuously for 24 hours and travel more than 3,100 miles (5,000 km) at speeds in excess of 125 mph (200 kph).

A dragster's rear spoiler creates downforce, while its sleek shape prevents drag.

RACING CAR

The Indianapolis 500

The Indianapolis Motor Speedway circuit was originally built in 1909 as a tar-and-gravel track and year-round testing facility for the car industry, which was growing rapidly in Indiana at the beginning of the 20th century. The idea was that people watching these small racing events would be so impressed with the cars that they would head to the car showrooms to buy one for themselves.

The track was later paved with over 3 million bricks, and the first Indianapolis 500 was held at the circuit in May, 1911. Ray Harroun beat the other 39 drivers in the field, winning the race with an average speed of 75 mph (120 kph). Following the suspension of racing during World War II, the Indianapolis Speedway track was sold to Anton Hulman Jr in 1945. Hulman spent millions of dollars improving the venue and turned the Indianapolis 500 into one of the greatest spectacles in motor racing.

Penske Racing is one of the most successful teams in Indianapolis 500 history. The team's owner, Roger Penske, is a former racing champion and the 1962 New York Times Driver of

Former racing champion and Indy team owner Roger Penske.

the Year. The Penske team first competed at Indianapolis in 1969 and soon became the team to beat!

When the drivers hear the words: "Gentlemen, start your engines!", they drive a complete circuit before beginning the race with a rolling start.

An Indy 500 racing car.

The car should be assembled in numerical order. Dotted lines shown on the pictures indicate how the model is scored and should be folded. Dotted lines do not appear on the model. Adult help may be required.

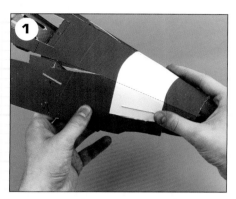

1. Take the Front Body and hold it face up. Bend all the scored edges downwards to make the whole structure more flexible.

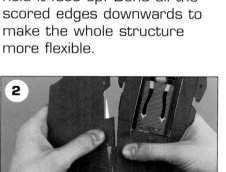

2. Look for the two flaps numbered 1. Firmly push the middle section of the body towards the outer to close the gap between both pieces numbered 1.

3. Lay both tabs flat at the back to secure. Repeat with the flaps numbered 2.

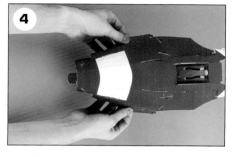

4. Hold the Front Body face up, and fold its tabs numbered 3 and 4 downwards.

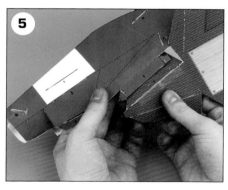

5. Take the Floor Assembly and, holding it face down, fold tabs numbered 3 and 4 upwards. Fix the Front Body to the Floor Assembly by pushing tab 3 through slot 3 as shown. Repeat this process with tab and slot 4.

6. Take the Front Left Rods piece and hold it face up. Fold the main flaps downwards.

7. Fold the small tabs either side of the numbers 5 and 6 downwards.

8. Push tab number 5 into slot number 5 on the Front Body and, once through, open up the small tabs to secure it in place. Repeat with tab and slot number 6. Repeat this process with the Front Right Rods, with the numbers 7 and 8 on it.

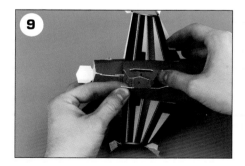

9. To pull the front of the car together, place the tab with number 9 on it into the number 9 slot. Open up the smaller flaps to secure once it is through the slot. Repeat this process with the tab and slot numbered 10.

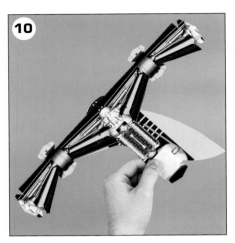

10. Hold the Rear Rods and Engine piece face up, and fold down all the scored edges.

11. Turn the Floor Assembly white side up and push tab 11 on the Rear Rods and Engine through slot 11.

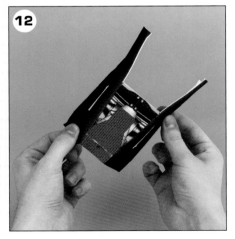

12. Holding the Gear Box and Rod Connect Assembly face up, fold all the scored edges to make it more flexible.

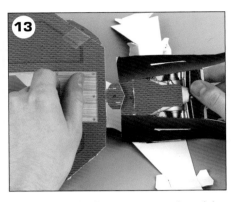

13. Turn it face up, and guide the tab numbered 12 on the Floor Assembly into the slot numbered 12 as shown.

14. Pull tab 13 on the Rear Rods and Engine piece over to slot into the number 13 slot on the Gear Box and Rod Connect Assembly, and open up the small flaps to secure it in place. Repeat with tab and slot number 14.

15. Fold down the flaps 15 and 16 on the Rear Rods and Engine, and then push them into the slots numbered 15 and 16 on the Gear Box and Rod Connect Assembly.

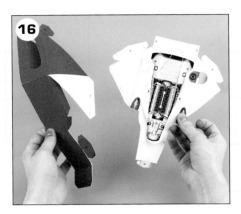

16. Take the Right Side Panel and Rear Body pieces, and fold all the scored lines to make them more flexible.

17. Holding both pieces face up, push tab 17 on the Rear Body into slot 17 on the Right Side Panel, as shown. Open up the small flaps to secure it.

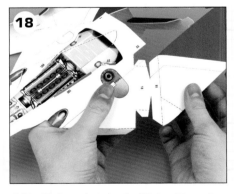

18. Take the Left Side Panel and, again, fold all the scored lines to make it more flexible. Repeat the same thing as you did for the Right Side Panel but this time with the tabs and slots numbered 18.

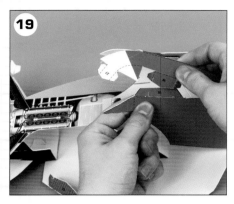

19. On the Front Body push tab 19 into slot 19 opening up the smaller tabs to secure it in place. Repeat with tab and slot 20.

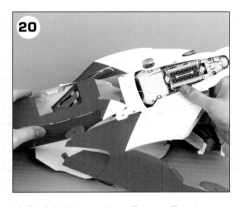

20. Holding the Rear Body face up, carefully guide it towards the piece of the car containing the Front Body.

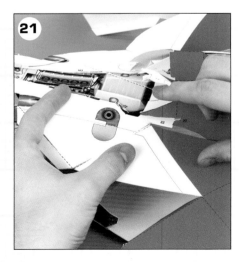

21. Slide slots 21 and 22 into slots 21 and 22 on the Front Body.

22. Push tab 23 into slot 23 and repeat with tabs and slots 24, 25, 26, 27 and 28. Remember to open up the small flaps to secure them in place.

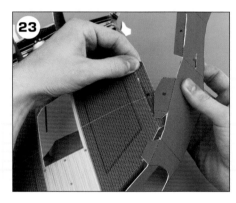

23. Push tab 29 on the Left Side Panel down into slot 29 on the Floor Assembly, securing the tab inside the car.

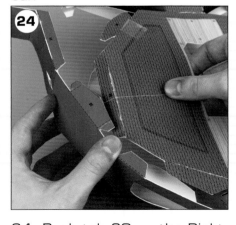

24. Push tab 30 on the Right Side Panel into slot 30 on the Floor Assembly, again making sure that all tabs are opened on the inside of the car.

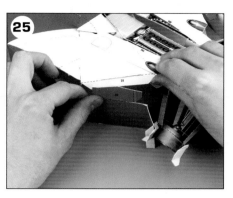

25. Push tab 31 on the Right Side Panel into slot 31 on the Rear Body.

26. Now push tab 32 on the Left Side Panel into slot 32 on the Rear Body. Open the tab to secure it, as before. Make sure the scored flaps around the sides are tucked in.

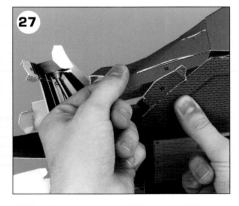

27. Push tabs 33 and 34 on the Floor Assembly into their respective slots on the side panels. Make sure that the rear tabs on the left and right body panels are tucked in.

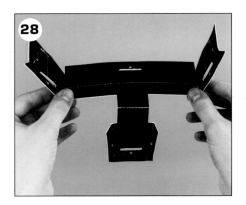

28. Fold the scored lines on the Rear Wing and Rear Wing Assembly 1 as shown. Fold the two large flaps inwards on the Rear Wing Assembly 1.

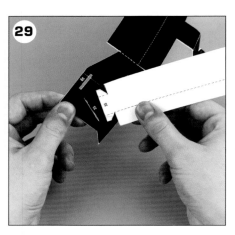

29. Push tabs 35 and 36 on the Rear Wing into their respective slots on the Rear Wing Assembly 1.

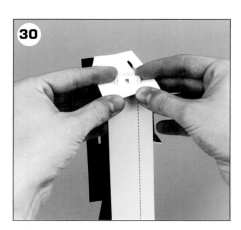

30. Remember to open out the smaller tabs to secure.

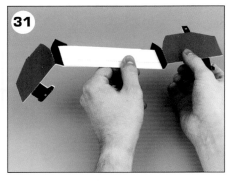

31. Take the Rear Wing Assembly 2. Fold all the scored lines to make it more flexible.

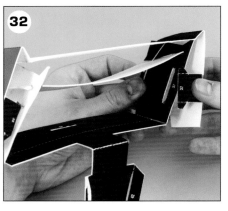

32. Place the Rear Wing Assembly 2 on the top of Rear Wing Assembly 1, pushing tab 37 through slot 37 and then wrapping the whole tab to the inside of the wing. Repeat this with tab and slot 38 opening the small flaps to secure once in place.

33. Take tab 39 and wrap it around to push into slot 39. Repeat with tab and slot 40.

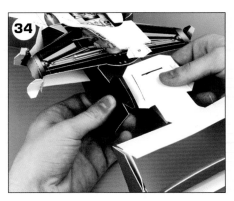

34. Attach the rear wing onto the body of the car by pushing tabs 41 and 42 on the Gear Box and Rod Connect Assembly into slots 41 and 42 on the Rear Wing Assembly.

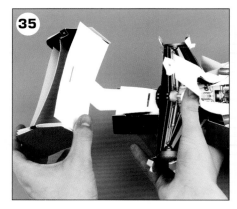

35. Once connected, fold the whole rear wing over so the two slots numbered 43 line up one above the other.

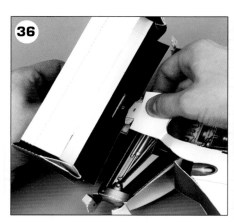

36. Tab 43 can then be pushed through both of these slots.

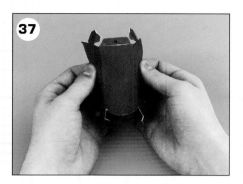

37. Hold the Front Nose face up, and fold down all the scored edges to make it flexible.

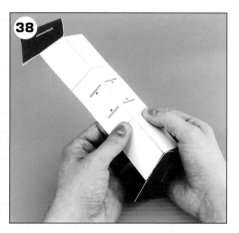

38. Fold the Front Wing 1 piece in half so that slots 44 and 45 lay over the second slots numbered 44 and 45.

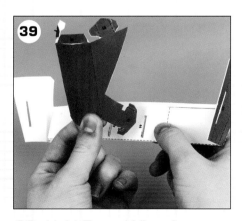

39. Hold Front Wing 1 as shown. Push tab 44 on the Front Nose as far as the notch into slots 44 on Front Wing 1. Repeat with tab and slots 45.

40. Take the Front Wing 2 piece and fold the scored lines. Fold over tab 46 and push it into slot 46 on Front Wing 1 as shown. Open out the tab to secure it in place. Align the notches into the back of the Front Nose. Repeat with tab and slot 47.

41. Attach this nose section to the main car by pushing tab 48 on the Front Body into slot 48 on the Front Nose.

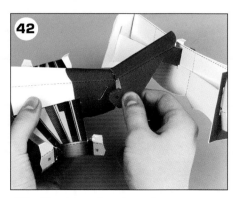

42. Secure further by pushing tabs 49 and 50 into their respective slots.

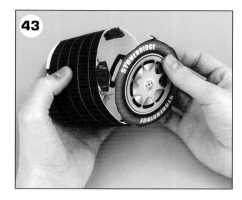

43. Take the Front Left Wheel Middle Part and prepare tabs 51 to 59. Push tabs 51 to 54 into slots 51 to 54 on the Front Left Wheel Inside Part. Push tabs 55 to 58 into slots 55 to 58 on the Front Left Wheel Outside Part.

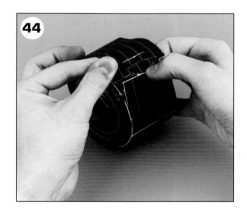

44. Push tab 59 into slot 59 to complete the circular shape of the wheel.

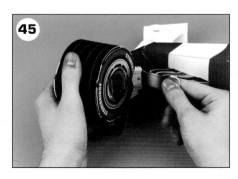

45. Fix this wheel to the main body of the car by pushing tabs 60 and 61 on the Front Left Rods into the slots 60 and 61 on the wheel.

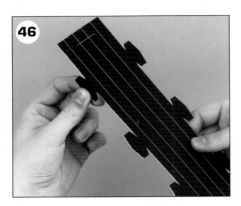

46. The next wheel to be completed is the Front Right Wheel. Take the Front Right Wheel Middle Part. Holding it face up, prepare tabs 62 to 70.

47. Slot the tabs 62 to 65 into the slots 62 to 65 on the Front Right Wheel Inside Part remembering to open up the small flaps once through the slot to secure.

48. Then push tabs 66 to 69 on the Front Right Wheel Outside Part through the slots 66 to 69 on the Front Right Wheel Middle Part.

49. Push tab 70 into slot 70 to complete the circular shape of the wheel.

50. Fix this wheel to the main body of the car by pushing tabs 71 and 72 on the Front Right Rods into the slots 71 and 72 on the wheel.

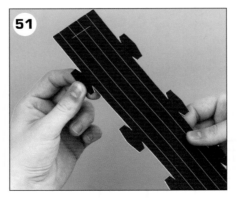

51. For the Rear Right Wheel, take the Rear Right Wheel Middle Part. Holding it face up, prepare tabs 73 to 81.

52. Slot the tabs 73 to 76 into the slots 73 to 76 on the Rear Right Wheel Inside Part, securing by flattening the smaller tabs once through the slot.

53. Push tabs 77 to 80 through their corresponding tabs on the Rear Right Wheel Outside Part.

54. Complete the wheel by pushing tab 81 through slot 81.

55. Fix the wheel onto the main body of the car by pushing tabs 82 and 83 on the Rear Rods and Engine part into the slots.

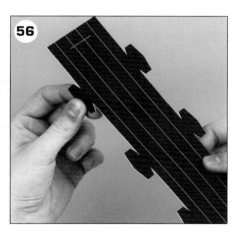

56. For the final wheel, take the Rear Left Wheel Middle Part and prepare the tabs.

57. Slot tabs 84 to 87 into the corresponding slots on the Rear Left Wheel Inside Part, and secure by opening the tabs once through the slots.

58. Push tabs 88 to 91 through their corresponding tabs on the Rear Left Wheel Outside Part and secure.

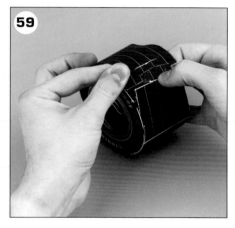

59. To complete your final wheel, push tab 92 through slot 92.

60. To fix the wheel onto the car, push tabs 93 and 94 on the Rear Rods and Engine part into slots 93 and 94 on the wheel.

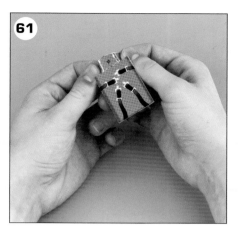

61. Fold the scored edges of the Seat and Seatbelts piece as shown.

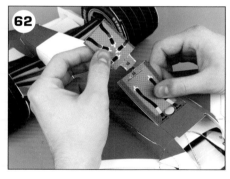

62. Push the seat into position in the main car by lifting up the seat with the slot marked 95 and pushing the tab down through the slot, then securing. Push the seat back down into the car.

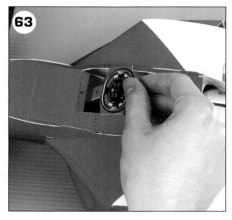

63. Push tab 96 on the Steering Wheel through slot 96 on the main car.

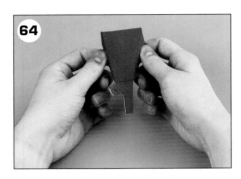

64. Take the Rear Wheel Cover Left and, holding it face upwards, bend along all the scored lines.

65. Push tab 97 into slot 97 on the main car as shown.

66. Repeat with the Rear Wheel Cover Right with tab and slot 98.

67. Take the final piece, the Engine Cover, and bend all the scored lines to make it flexible.

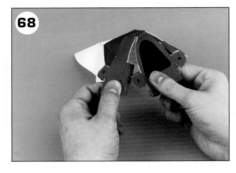

68. Push tab 99 into the slot numbered 99 and tab 100 into slot 100. Secure by opening out the tabs.

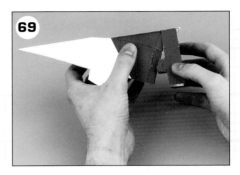

69. Push tab 101 through slot 101 and tab 102 through slot 102. Secure.

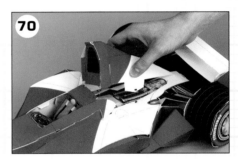

70. Fix the Engine Cover to the car by pushing tabs 103 and 104 into slots 103 and 104 on the top of the car.

Congratulations! You have completed your model.

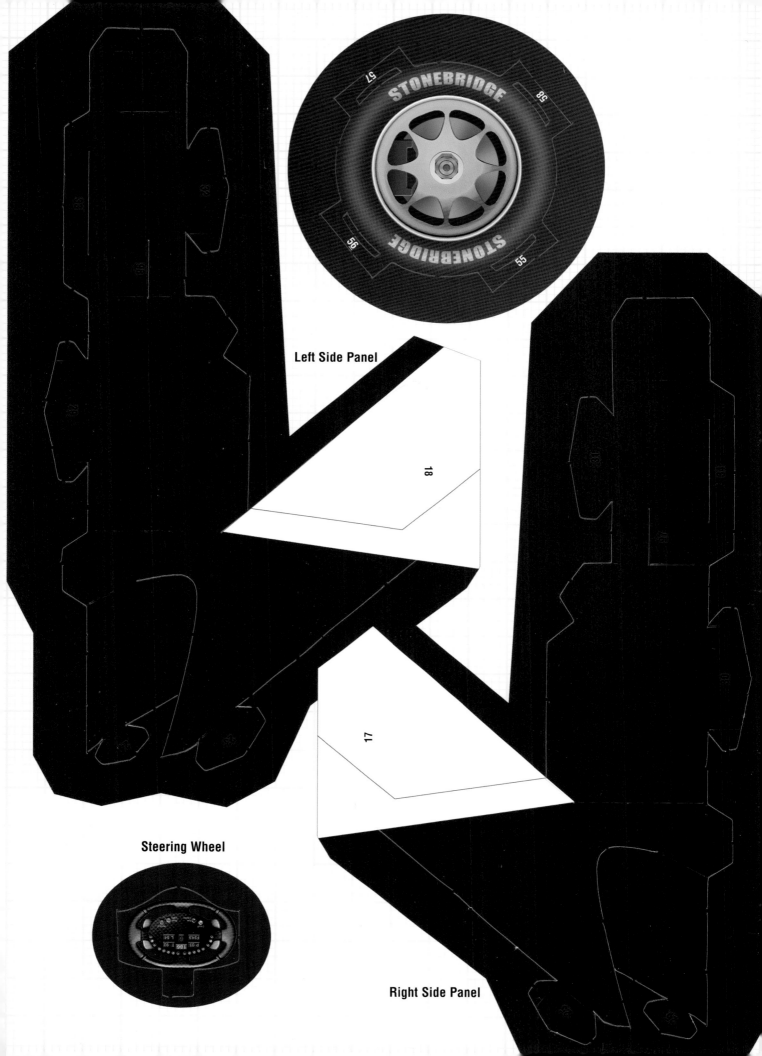

Left Side Panel

Steering Wheel

Right Side Panel

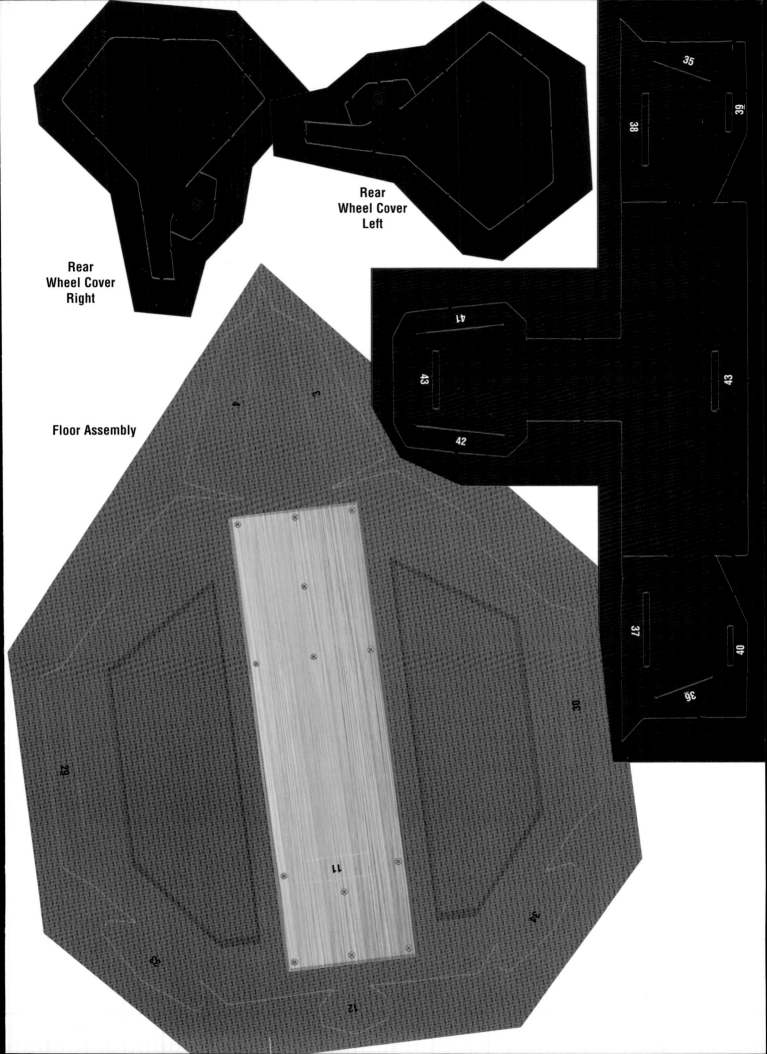

Rear
Wheel Cover
Left

Rear
Wheel Cover
Right

Floor Assembly

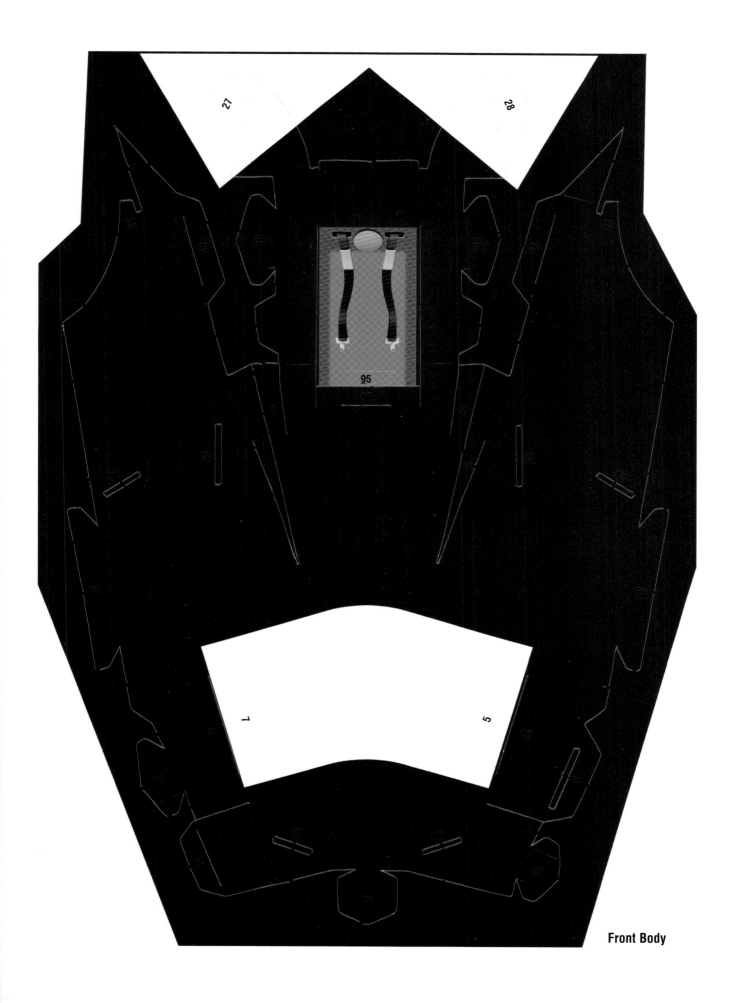

Front Body

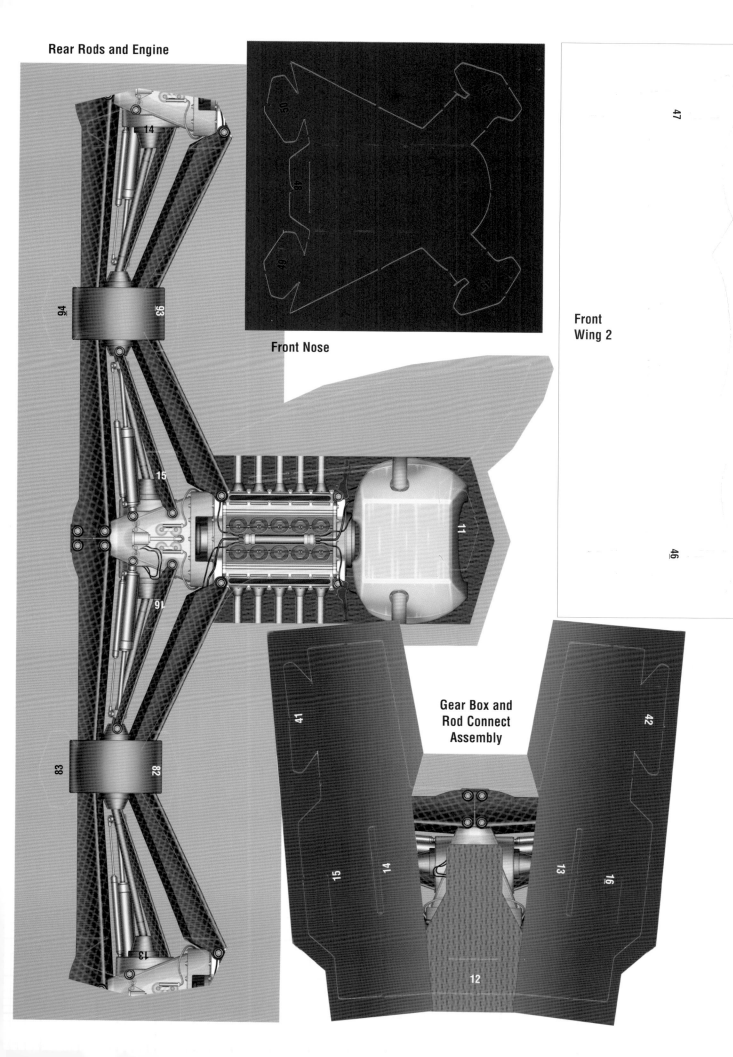

Rear Rods and Engine

Front Nose

Front
Wing 2

Gear Box and
Rod Connect
Assembly

Front Right Wheel Middle Part

70

66
65

67
64

68
63

69
62

70

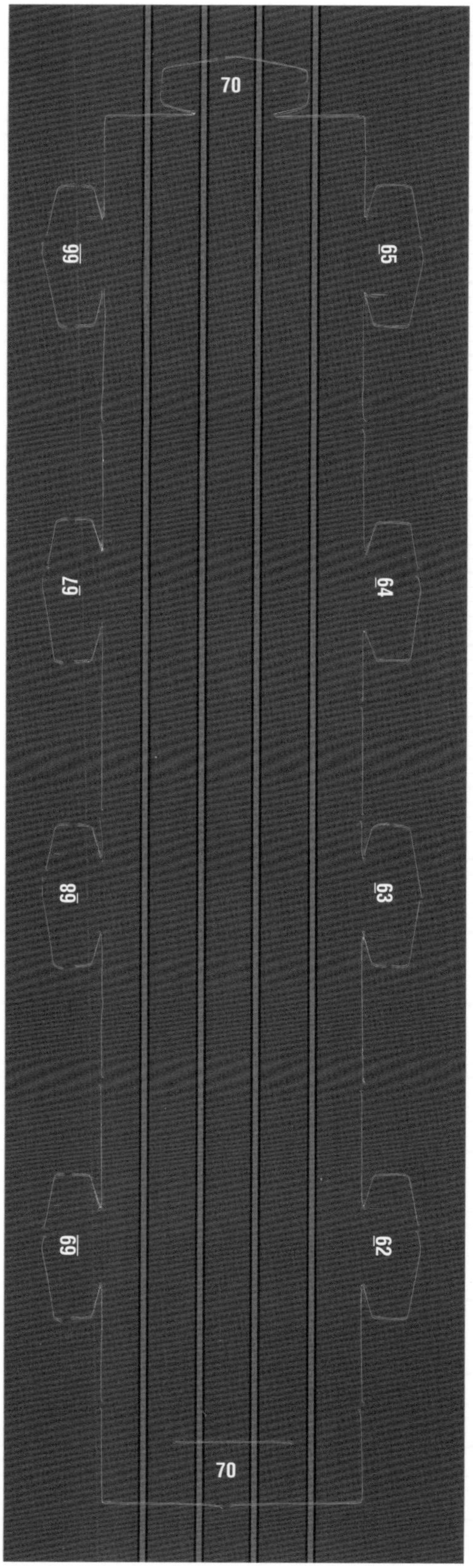

Rear Right Wheel Middle Part

81

77
76

78
75

79
74

80
73

81

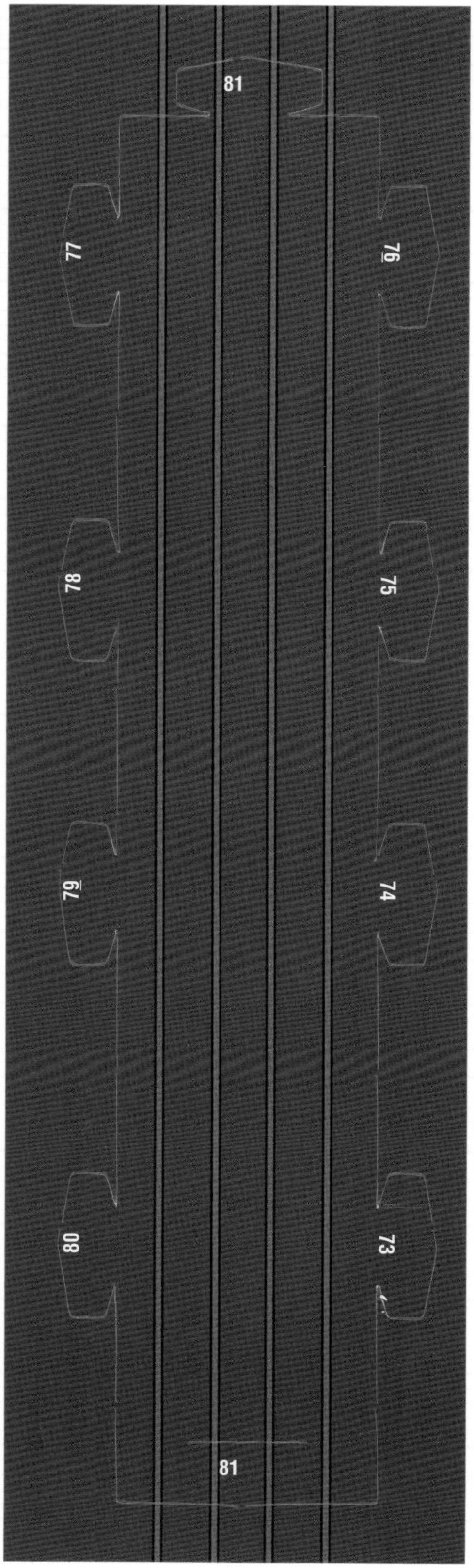

Rear Left Wheel Middle Part

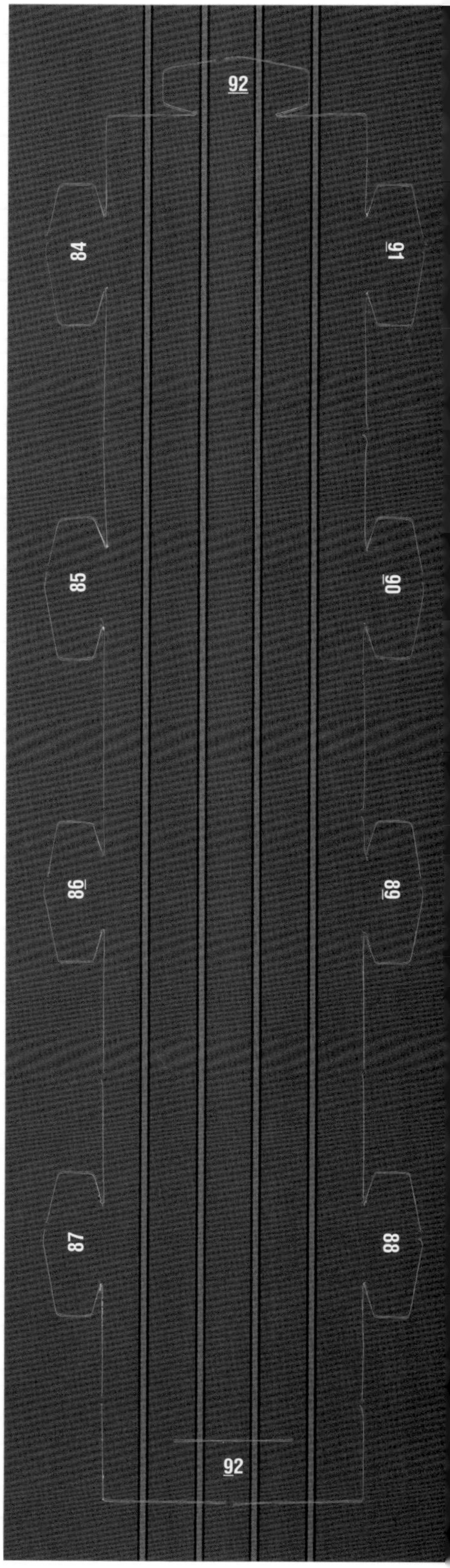

92

84
91

85
90

86
89

87
88

92

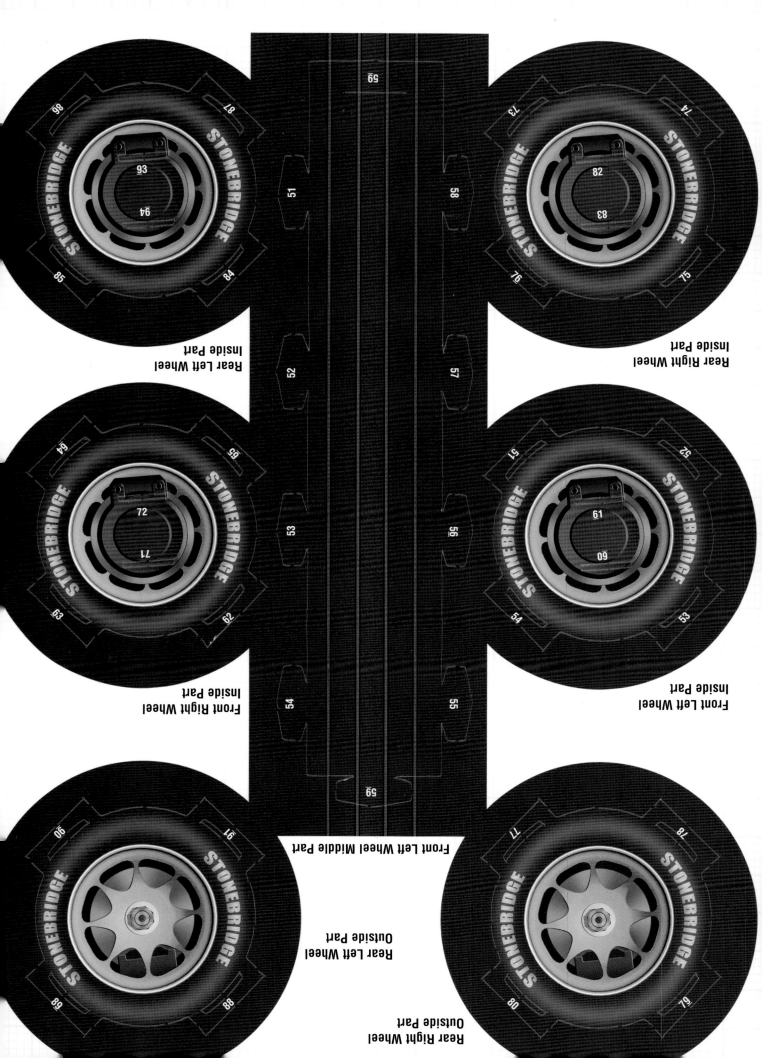

Rear Left Wheel
Inside Part

Rear Right Wheel
Inside Part

Front Right Wheel
Inside Part

Front Left Wheel
Inside Part

Front Left Wheel Middle Part

Rear Left Wheel
Outside Part

Rear Right Wheel
Outside Part

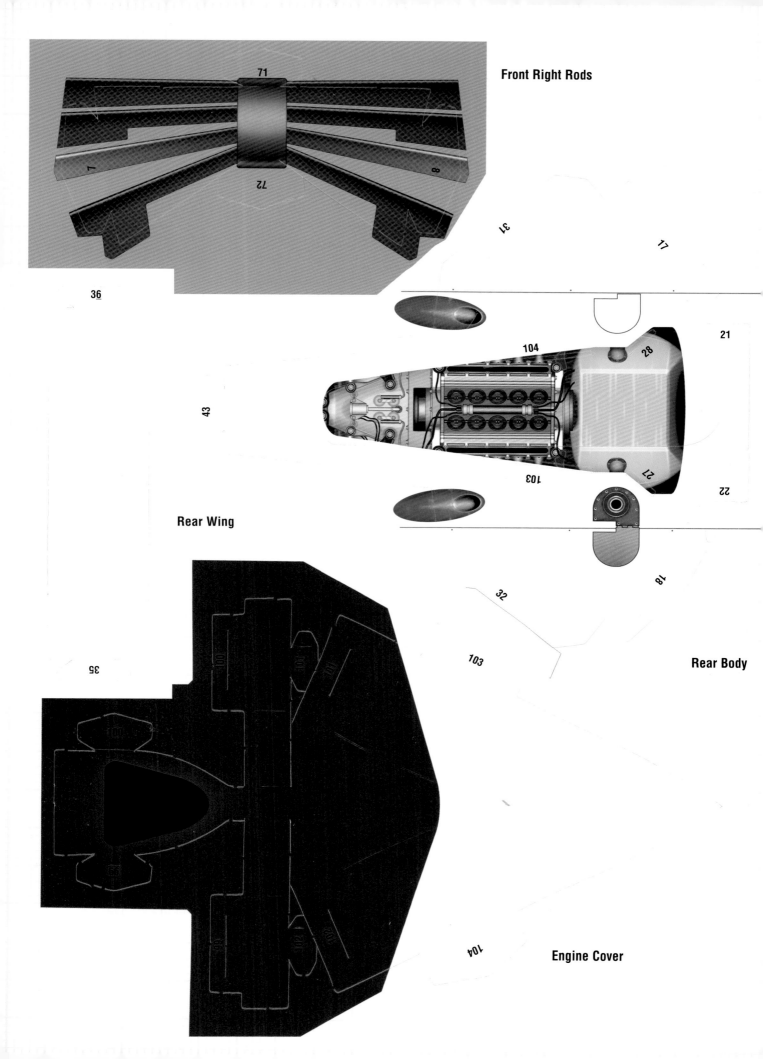

Front Right Rods

71

7

8

72

31

17

36

21

28

104

22

43

103

27

18

Rear Wing

32

103

Rear Body

35

104

Engine Cover